Toronto Sketches 11

MIKE FILEY

Toronto
Sketches

11

DUNDURN
TORONTO

Editor: Allison Hirst
Design: Jesse Hooper
Printer: Webcom

Library and Archives Canada Cataloguing in Publication

Filey, Mike, 1941-
    Toronto sketches 11 / Mike Filey.

"The way we were" columns from the Toronto Sunday Sun.
Issued also in electronic formats.
ISBN 978-1-4597-0763-4

    1. Toronto (Ont.)--History. I. Title. II. Title: Toronto sketches eleven.

FC3097.4.F5498 2012   971.3'541   C2012-903226-3

1   2   3   4   5   16   15   14   13   12

We acknowledge the support of the **Canada Council for the Arts** and the **Ontario Arts Council** for our publishing program. We also acknowledge the financial support of the **Government of Canada** through the **Canada Book Fund** and **Livres Canada Books**, and the **Government of Ontario** through the **Ontario Book Publishing Tax Credit** and the **Ontario Media Development Corporation**.

Care has been taken to trace the ownership of copyright material used in this book. The author and the publisher welcome any information enabling them to rectify any references or credits in subsequent editions.

J. Kirk Howard, President

Printed and bound in Canada.

VISIT US AT
Dundurn.com | Definingcanada.ca | @dundurnpress | Facebook.com/dundurnpress

Dundurn	Gazelle Book Services Limited	Dundurn
3 Church Street, Suite 500	White Cross Mills	2250 Military Road
Toronto, Ontario, Canada	High Town, Lancaster, England	Tonawanda, NY
M5E 1M2	LA1 4XS	U.S.A. 14150

For my proofreader,
spell–checker,
best friend,
and wife,
Yarmila

Contents

Author's Note

The origin of Toronto Sketches, "The Way We Were," this being Volume 11 in the series, goes back to the late summer of 1971 when the editor of the real estate section of Toronto's now-defunct *Telegram* newspaper asked me to provide a few lines of text and a couple of photographs to fill space that had resulted from an insufficient number of ads being sold. This arrangement went on for a few months until the good old *Tely* finally folded. Within days, a new kid, the *Toronto Sun*, appeared in news boxes around town. Perhaps desperate for material to fill the struggling tabloid, the *Toronto Sun* made my columns a semi-regular feature. Then, with the introduction of the *Sunday Sun* in 1973, "The Way We Were" became a weekly feature. And the rest, they say, is history — at least eleven volumes' worth so far!

Many of my earlier columns have been reproduced in volumes 1 through 10 of this series. The columns in this book originally appeared in 2010, 2011, and 2012. Appended to each column is the date it first appeared as well as any relevant material that may have surfaced since that date (indicated by an asterisk).

Dancing Days of Yesteryear

During the first half of the last century, Toronto could boast that it was home to some of the most popular dance halls in the entire country. Places such as the Silver Slipper north of Lakeshore Road on the east bank of the Humber River, the Club Esquire and Club Top Hat (located in the same building, although at different times, at Sunnyside Amusement Park on Humber Bay), the nearby and recently restored Palais Royale, the Masonic Temple at Yonge and Davenport, the Club 12 at 12 Adelaide Street East, and the Embassy at the northeast corner of Bloor and Bellair. This latter club was unique in that it had a specially designed dance floor that would sway with the dancers. It also opened as a very exclusive private club modelled after several others with the same name located in New York and London. Unfortunately, our Embassy Club went bankrupt after only a few years, but it did stick around as a regular dance venue until the 1960s.

While most of Toronto's dance halls eventually went out of business due to changing trends, the one that was arguably the best known and at the time still doing a brisk business, was destroyed at the hands of an arsonist.

Proposed in the mid-1920s by a group of English businessmen, the building started out as just one component of a mammoth pleasure pier complex that would jut out into Lake Ontario from the Etobicoke side of the Humber River. The dance hall part of the project would accommodate three thousand couples in a ballroom that covered thirty thousand square feet and could be converted to a skating rink in the winter. Other buildings on the pier would include a 1,400-seat theatre and a large bandstand, as well as restaurants and souvenir stores. The complex would be known as the Palace Pier, a name it took from the extremely popular Palace Pier located in Brighton, England.

For a variety of reasons, the vast majority of which were brought on by the Great Depression and the resulting failure to sell a sufficient number of ten-dollar shares to the cash-strapped public to cover the million-dollar cost of the total project, the only thing Torontonians got in the end was the ballroom.

Looking east along the Queen Elizabeth Highway toward downtown Toronto from above the Christie Brown factory on Lake Shore Boulevard West, circa 1954. The biscuit company's water tank, which is still there, is at the bottom of the photo. Near the top of the photo and jutting out into Lake Ontario at the mouth of the Humber River is the Palace Pier, which went up in flames on January 7, 1963.

Though initially built as a place where couples could dance to the sounds of the big bands (Canada's Trump Davidson and Ellis McClintock were favourites), the Palace Pier was also used as a roller skating rink, a public auditorium, and as a venue for wrestling and boxing matches.

But it all came to an end early on the morning of January 7, 1963, when flames swept rapidly through the old building. Toronto lost one of its great landmarks that day.

At the top right of the accompanying photo, you can see the Palace Pier jutting out into the lake. In the foreground is the Lion Monument that was erected at the junction of Toronto's Lake Shore Boulevard and the Queen Elizabeth Highway (QEW) coincident with the dedication of the "Queen E" by the Queen Mother in 1939. When the highway was widened in the mid-1970s, the monument was moved to a safer location on the east bank of the Humber River, south of what was previously known as the QEW, but since 1997 has been part of the Gardiner Expressway.

January 3, 2010

Remember Kids, Safety First

When I was just a young whippersnapper (when was the last time you heard that term?) attending John Fisher Public School in North Toronto, one event that became one of my most vivid memories (in addition to listening to bird call imitations by the school principal, whose name was Austin and who didn't seem to have a first name — teachers never did) was the arrival of a couple of police officers in the company of one "Elmer, the Safety Elephant." The arrival of this trio usually meant the school was about to receive the Elmer pennant to fly under the Union Jack on the flag pole, a flag that would signify no student had been in a traffic accident for a period of thirty days. However, on more sombre occasions the police would be there to take it down if one of the students had been injured, or worse.

Elmer was the brainchild of Toronto mayor Robert Saunders, who got the idea while visiting Detroit, where a very successful child safety program had been in place for several years. The mayor got several editors at the *Evening Telegram* newspaper interested in developing a similar program for Toronto. It was decided that here the safety message would be promoted by a mascot in the form of a cartoon elephant.

Why an elephant, you ask? Well, because an elephant never forgets, and in this case Elmer never forgets the rules of pedestrian safety, and nor should the city's schoolchildren. To complete the picture, quite literally, an artist from the Disney studios developed the image that quickly became the Elmer that children came to recognize and obey. Elmer, accompanied by a couple of real live police officers (anyone remember Inspectors Vern Page and Charles Pearsall?) would visit the city's public schools, where the trio would emphasize pedestrian traffic safety. (By the way, there's a great video available online at *www.cbc.ca/ archives/categories/lifestyle/living/general-15/an-elephant-brings-safety-to-our-schools.html*.)

"Blinky, the Talking Police Car."

By the mid-1960s, a new generation of school kids needed something a little more expressive than a flag and a three-foot-high model of an elephant. So, up stepped Metro Toronto Police Sergeant Roy Wilson with an idea. He approached the popular radio station CHUM as a possible sponsor of an animated police car that the officer would both design and help build. The station thought it was a great idea, and it wasn't long before "Blinky" was born. At first the car's actions were quite simple, but as the potential of such an educational tool became apparent, improvements were made. Soon Blinky didn't just blink, he could wink and his "voice" was more audible. He visited shopping malls and appeared in a variety of parades. Over the years, Elmer and his pal Blinky have encouraged thousands of children to understand and respect the hazards associated with living in a busy city like Toronto.

January 24, 2010

Blinky's creator, former Toronto police officer Roy Wilson (left), and retired inspector and force historian Mike Sale. Wilson sold his "Blinky" patent to the department for one dollar.

On a Wing and a Prayer

In 2010, the new Toronto Island Airport ferry was christened *Marilyn Bell 1* in honour of the former Toronto schoolgirl who became the first person to swim Lake Ontario. Marilyn, who was just sixteen years old at the time, accomplished the task on September 9, 1954. She completed the torturous forty-mile crossing from Youngstown, New York, to the break wall south of the Boulevard Club in Toronto's west end in just under twenty-one hours.

Flight Lieutenant David Hornell, VC, by war artist Paul Goranson.

This painting by artist Graham Wragg depicts Hornell's PBY-5 Canso flying boat in its death throes following an attack on a German submarine off the coast of northern Scotland in late June, 1944.

Now Marilyn Bell-Dilascio, and living in New York, the Canadian heroine did the honours, although out of deference to the environment she poured the traditional champagne over the ship's name plate rather than smashing the bottle over the bow.

Coincident with the naming of the new vessel and the change of the airport's name to the Billy Bishop Toronto Island Airport (over the years since it opened in 1939 the facility has been known as Port George V Airport, Toronto Island Airport, and, most recently, Toronto City Centre Airport), the Toronto Port Authority officials decided to rename the existing ferry, as well. It has been known since its arrival in the fall of 2006 by the rather mundane title *TCCA1*.

Following a public contest, which saw the swimmer's name selected as the name of the new ferry, the next most popular choice and the one that would be affixed to the older vessel was that of David Hornell. And while the former had over the years become a well-known name, the latter was less so.

The Toronto Island Airport ferry *TCCA I* was recently renamed in honour of David Hornell, VC.

David Hornell was born on Toronto Island on January 26, 1910, and subsequently moved to Mimico (a western suburb of Toronto), where he attended a local public school before moving on to high school. Following the outbreak of the Second World War in the fall of 1939, David joined the Royal Canadian Air Force (RCAF) and received his wings in September 1941. He served on both Canadian coasts before being shipped overseas. It was while on patrol in his PBY-5 Canso flying boat off the coast of northern Scotland that the crew spotted a surfaced German U-boat. Pressing the attack, Flight Lieutenant Hornell's aircraft was badly damaged by shelling from the enemy submarine and soon the entire starboard side of the aircraft was in flames. Nevertheless, Hornell and his crew continued the attack and ultimately destroyed the submarine. But they then found themselves in trouble. With incredible dexterity, the pilot crash-landed the severely damaged aircraft, and although almost blind, he determinedly encouraged his crew to fight off the notion that they all were doomed. After nearly twenty-one hours taking turns in the only useable rubber lifeboat, the crew was rescued. But it was too late for the badly injured David Hornell, and he soon succumbed to his injuries.

January 31, 2010

Never-Ending Roadwork

I think I'm correct when I suggest that the city street that has received the most attention by the media over the past few years is St. Clair Avenue, and in particular the part that stretches west from Yonge Street. And there's really no need to repeat the almost unanimous consensus that the construction of the dedicated streetcar right-of-way along this street could have been done faster, cheaper, and with less disruption of the neighbourhoods involved. People cleverer than I am have told anyone who will listen (as well as some who won't) just how it should have been done in the first place.

Actually, this brief preamble leads us to the subject of this chapter. The construction of the new St. Clair right-of-way isn't the first (or even the second or third) time this broad thoroughfare (which was initially a muddy and often impassable concession road blazed through the forest exactly one-and-one-quarter miles north of Bloor Street) has been subjected to major road work.

In fact, in the 1911 City of Toronto Archives photo (opposite), the street is undergoing the first of those seemingly interminable construction projects. And you can almost hear the neighbours wondering just what impact the arrival of the electric streetcar was going to have on their pastoral way of life. Under a magnifying glass, I think I can even see a "Save Our St. Clair" poster.

Looking east on St. Clair Avenue from just east of Dufferin Street, 1911. Note the newly built Oakwood Collegiate in the background on the right.

The same view almost one hundred years later.

In the photo, rails are just being laid, but soon the streetcar would become a permanent fact of life for those living out on St. Clair West. But you'll notice there's something missing — the good old TTC. Another decade would pass before what was originally known as the Toronto Transportation Commission would take over responsibility for the city's public transit needs. When this photo was taken, the new St. Clair streetcar line was just being built by the city's Works Department. The reason it became the department's project was because the private company that looked after the transportation needs of the rest of the city steadfastly refused to build tracks and operate a streetcar service in a suburban area of Toronto that they said wouldn't generate any money. And unlike today's municipally owned TTC, for the private company the reasoning was sound. The object of providing transit service was simple — to make money, and lots of it, for the company owners and its shareholders.

And so it was that when the first streetcars on St. Clair began running on August 25, 1913, they were operated by the city, while other streetcar lines remained under private ownership until the TTC took over on September 1, 1921.

A brief aside: Some readers may recall a time when those in the know claimed that electric streetcars were "dinosaurs," and that by 1980 Toronto would be rid of them. In fact, they said the St. Clair route should be one of the first lines to vanish. Not only was the TTC smart enough to keep them, but many Torontonians have come to embrace the streetcar, as have several American cities and their citizens. And, in a strange turn of events, the TTC has recently ordered a large number of new, state-of-the-art streetcars to replace its aging fleet of CLRVs and ALRVs (Canadian and Articulated Light Rail Vehicles).

Worldwide, electric vehicles are seen as the way of the future for numerous smog- and traffic-choked cities.

February 7, 2010

Toronto EMS Has Come a Long Way

One afternoon I was sitting in my local Tim Hortons reading the *Sun* (what else) and sipping on a hot chocolate, when all of a sudden several EMS paramedics and a number of firefighters rushed in. Together they began assisting an elderly gentleman in a nearby booth who was obviously in some distress. Within minutes they had him stabilized, on a stretcher, out the door, and on his way to the hospital. While I'll never know the final outcome of this little drama, I hope I will receive the same quick and skilled response from the ladies and gentlemen of Toronto Fire Services and Toronto's Emergency Medical Services if I'm ever faced with a similar crisis.

The event prompted me to look into the history of ambulance service in our city. Thanks to copious research that has been done by EMS historian Bruce Newton, the facts have been neatly presented on the department's website (*torontoems.ca/mainsite/about/history.html*).

In the city's earliest days, a form of ambulance service (and the term "service" is a bit of a stretch) was provided by local cab drivers and the odd Good Samaritan who would happen upon infectious, ill, or injured citizens and haul them off to the city's only hospital. It wasn't until the 1870s that the city fathers of the growing metropolis recognized their obligation to provide this necessary service. So they contracted a local undertaker to provide something a little more dependable.

Toronto Police Department horse-drawn ambulance, circa 1888.

This ambulance was given to Toronto General Hospital by Sir John Eaton, circa 1912.

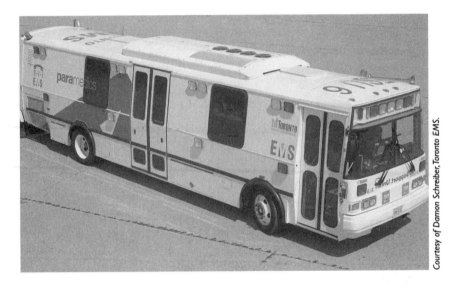

A modern Toronto EMS multi-patient ambulance bus.

Over the next few years, and thanks to the generosity of department store magnate Sir John Eaton, the Toronto General Hospital began providing an ambulance service. So, too, did the police department, followed by the city's Department of Health. Seeing this as a new source of income, many of the city's undertaking establishments got into the ambulance business as well, and by the time the government stepped in and streamlined the activities, "customers" had their choice of twenty-seven different ambulance services. Anyone remember Kane, Ogden, or Hallowell ambulances racing along city streets?

Interestingly, two tragedies prompted government officials to at least consider taking some form of action. The first was the fire aboard the passenger ship SS *Noronic*, which destroyed the ship as it was moored at the foot of Yonge Street in the fall of 1949. The lack of proper communications, as well as far too few proper ambulances, resulted in many badly burned victims being transported to the downtown hospitals in regular taxi cabs.

Then, in November 1963, the city's young mayor, Donald Summerville, suffered a serious heart attack while playing an exhibition hockey game in west Toronto. Because the closest ambulance was near Weston and the venue was outside its area of responsibility, and the next closest city ambulance took far too long get to the scene, the unfortunate mayor was beyond help by the time medical personnel arrived.

So finally, on February 12, 1975, all ambulance operations came under the jurisdiction of Metro Toronto's newly organized Department of Ambulance Services. Today, this important and quite literally life-saving function is carried out by Toronto EMS.

February 14, 2010

Life and Times of the SS Cayuga

Over the past several decades, several entrepreneurs have tried to reinstate some form of passenger ship service across Lake Ontario from the Port of Toronto. Two of the most recent attempts involved Russian-built hydrofoils to and from Queenston on the Niagara River and an Australian-built catamaran that operated between Toronto and Rochester.

The latter vessel, known as either the "Cat," the "Breeze," or officially as *The Spirit of Ontario*, made a number of runs during 2004 and 2005 before being removed from service and, after lengthy legal hassles, offered up for sale. Eventually, the renamed *Tangier Jet II* began a new career in the Strait of Gibraltar, ferrying passengers between Tarifa, Spain, and Tangier, Morocco.

As hard as people tried to make a success of their cross-lake passenger service, none was able to match the achievements of the Lake Ontario steamers of the early to mid-twentieth century. Most impressive were the Niagara boats with stirring names such as *Chippewa*, *Corona*, and *Cayuga*. Over the years this trio carried millions of travellers between Toronto and the Niagara River ports of Niagara-on-the-Lake, Queenston, and Lewiston, New York. But of all the Lake Ontario passenger ships, the one that many readers of my column will remember, and the one that remained in service the longest, was SS *Cayuga*.

Components of the almost 122-metre-long vessel with a carrying capacity of more than two thousand passengers were fabricated in the old Bertram Engine Works factory at the northeast corner of Bathurst and Front streets in Toronto (the building is still there). The actual assembly of the ship took place in the harbour just across the railway tracks to the southeast of the old West Gap.

In this 1954 photograph, Toronto's popular Lake Ontario cruise boat SS *Cayuga* is outbound through the East Gap on her way to ports on the Niagara River. At the time the ship was being operated by the newly formed Cayuga Steamship Company. After being given what would turn out to be an all-too-brief reprieve from the wrecker's cutting torch, *Cayuga*'s new owners offered cross-lake cruises for as low as $3.90 return.

The ship was christened on March 3, 1906, by Mary Osler, daughter of Edmund (later Sir Edmund) Osler, one of the directors of the new ship's owners, the Northern Navigation Company. Interestingly, Mary's niece, Phyllis Osler, would do the same honours four years later at the launch of the new island ferry, *Trillium*, owned by Edmond Osler's Toronto Ferry Company.

A little over a year passed before the SS *Cayuga*, perfectly fitted out and fresh from successful sea trials, began the Toronto–Niagara-on-the-Lake–Queenston–Lewiston, New York service. The date was June 7, and over the next half-century she carried passengers to and from Niagara, for a few years transporting recently enlisted young soldiers to the newly established military camp that had been hurriedly set up at Niagara-on-the-Lake following the outbreak of the First World War.

The amazingly popular ship operated on the route until 1952, when its owner, Canada Steamship Lines, decided to get out of the passenger business and devote all its efforts to moving freight. After being laid up for a couple of seasons, a group of enthusiasts purchased the vessel for its scrap value ($17,000), and in 1954 *Cayuga* was back in service under a new flag — that of the Cayuga Steamship Company. With the highways to Niagara becoming increasingly congested, it was hoped that both Canadian and American tourists would find travelling to and from Toronto by boat was the better way.

Now, if only *Cayuga* could get a liquor licence …

But without that elusive licence, nostalgia and a crowded Queen Elizabeth Highway just weren't enough to guarantee the ship a prosperous new life. On Labour Day 1957, SS *Cayuga* made her final trip. The company was bankrupt and the future of the once-proud ship again seemed bleak.

Eventually the ship was purchased by a wrecking company, and plans were formulated that would see it return to service as either a floating hotel adjacent to the CNE or as a new waterfront restaurant similar to Captain John's *Jadran*. But it all came to nothing, and in 1960–61, after rusting away in Toronto Harbour, *Cayuga*'s days came to an end when it was unceremoniously scrapped.

Thousands of artifacts from *Cayuga* were saved and became part of the collection at the late, lamented Marine Museum of Upper Canada that was located in the historic Stanley Barracks on the CNE grounds. The collection was moved to a new location on Queen's Quay called The Pier, where visitors could relive the "good old days." But sadly this museum was also closed and today all those memories are stored out of sight in a city warehouse.

February 28, 2010

Crash Course in History

Shortly before 7:00 p.m. on the evening of November 17, 1904, street-car number 642, owned and operated by the city's private transportation provider, the Toronto Railway Company, was proceeding east along Queen Street. As it approached the Grand Trunk Railway's level crossing just past De Grassi Street, it became clear that something was wrong. Orders issued by the company required streetcars to approach all railway crossings at minimal speed, but for some reason number 642 was travelling well in excess of this limit. Suddenly, the crossing gates began to drop — a Montreal-bound train was approaching. Motorman Willis Armstrong tried, but he couldn't bring his vehicle to a stop in time. The heavy steam engine smashed into the wooden streetcar, reducing it to kindling. Two passengers were killed instantly and a third died later in hospital. A dozen others suffered a variety of injuries.

Motorman Armstrong was charged with manslaughter and held in jail for several weeks until inspection of the ill-fated streetcar's braking system proved his statement to police that the system was totally ineffectual. Inspection also determined that a secondary safety feature installed by the company, something called a "Scotch dog," which, when the crossing gates dropped, caused a five-inch-long bolt to rise above the streetcar tracks and derail the car before it reached the railway tracks, was also deemed totally useless at the speed the car was travelling.

Officials recommended that the level crossing be eliminated and a railway bridge be built as soon as possible. The bridge opened twenty-three years later.

March 21, 2010

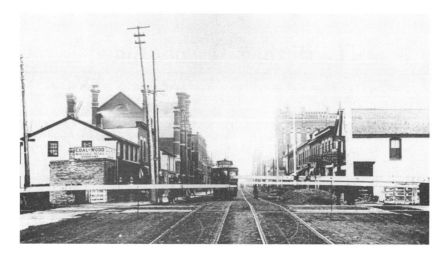

View of Queen Street, looking west from the Grand Trunk railway crossing between De Grassi and McGee streets, circa 1892. Note the early electric streetcar on the Lee route stopped at the crossing gate. This route, from the St. Lawrence Market along King and Queen Streets to Lee Avenue in the Beach was only in service for short time.

A similar view in 2010.

The Birth of Toronto Island

It was 1858 when one of Toronto's most treasured attractions, our own Toronto Island, first came into being. This historic event was recorded in the following day's *Globe* newspaper:

The Peninsula Hotel Washed Away

A disaster which has for some time been anticipated occurred yesterday morning (April 13) with the washing away of Mr. Quinn's hotel on the Island. The storm commenced early on the afternoon of the previous day (April 12) and towards night the breeze freshened, and continued blowing steadily from the north-east. Such was the fury of the tempest on the bay that serious fears were entertained that the hotel would be blown down, but it withstood the violence of the hurricane. Towards morning the waves were breaking on the beach in rear of the house and at about five o'clock the water made a complete breach over the Island, undermining the house and leaving it a total wreck, and at the same time **making a wide channel four or five feet in depth which will make**

a convenient eastern entrance to the harbour for vessels of light draught. Fortunately, Mr. Quinn, who was anticipating the cataclysm, succeeded in removing his family and the greater part of his furniture to a small dwelling which he had erected a short time ago, a little to the west of his late residence.

Before this severe storm wreaked havoc across the young city's waterfront, what was to suddenly become Toronto Island (while in this case "island" is a singular term, numerous large and small islands covering a total of 825 acres are involved) was originally nothing more than a series of long, sandy "fingers" of land known collectively as The Peninsula. This formation trailed westward from a swampy landmass at the east end of the harbour, an area originally called Ashbridge's Bay, then the Eastern Harbour Terminal District, and now simply as the Port Lands.

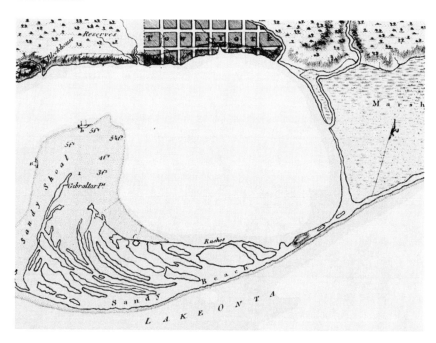

A map of the Town of York (renamed City of Toronto in 1834) sketched prior to the tremendous storm that struck the young city on April 13, 1858, that resulted in the creation of Toronto Island. Note the narrow and extremely vulnerable isthmus that connects the town with what would later become the island.

Geologists tell us that much of the material that made up those "fingers" actually originated as sand and rocks that over countless centuries had eroded from the weather-worn surfaces of the bluffs located a few miles east of the town site. (This geological feature was first referred to as the Scarborough Bluffs in the late 1700s by Governor Simcoe's wife, Elizabeth, soon after the couple's arrival to take up residence in the new Province of Upper Canada).

It was the counter-clockwise circulation of water on this side of the lake that resulted in this eroded material migrating in a westerly direction. Over time, sufficient quantities of silt and sand dropped out of the solution when met by the outflows from the Rouge, Don, and Humber watercourses to create a substrate to which, centuries later, newcomers to the area added harbour dredgings and construction debris, resulting in the much enlarged Toronto Island that we have today.

While the first breach in the narrow isthmus took place more than 150 years ago, it wasn't until this newly created channel was widened, made deeper, and stabilized over the next few years that it became a truly useful entrance and exit to and from Toronto Harbour.

April 11, 2010

The Eastern Channel had been in existence for less than half a century when a photographer captured these two ladies watching the passenger ships SS *City of Ottawa* and SS *Chicora*, a sailboat, and the tug *D.W. Crow* traverse Toronto Harbour's Eastern Channel.

Titanic's Toronto Connection

On April 18, 1912, the Cunard liner RMS (Royal Mail Ship) *Carpathia* arrived at the Port of New York carrying 705 survivors of one of the worst sea disasters in history: the sinking of the "unsinkable" RMS *Titanic*, which resulted in the loss of 1,503 of her passengers and crew. Among the survivors aboard *Carpathia* — Cunard's much smaller Atlantic liner, which had been bound for Mediterranean ports when it's crew had received the distress calls and without hesitation turned about and raced through miles and miles of thick pack ice to the scene of the disaster — was Toronto businessman and member of the Queen's Own Rifles of Canada, Major Arthur Peuchen, president of the Standard Chemical Company and a first-class passenger on the ill-fated White Star super liner. Peuchen had crossed the Atlantic dozens of times without incident. But this particular crossing was to change his life.

Peuchen's Toronto-based company had developed a highly efficient method of obtaining acetone from the distillation of wood. This chemical was a key component in the creation of cordite, a propellant used in the manufacture of artillery shells. For many, including Peuchen, the prospect of a major conflict erupting in Europe was both bad news (for obvious reasons) and good news, because if war broke out, millions of artillery shells would be needed — and tremendous quantities of cordite would be needed to propel those shells toward the enemy lines. Companies in the acetone-producing business would not only be regarded as patriotic, but they would reap great financial rewards for their stockholders as well.

Lacking large wooded areas (most having already been cut down), it was painfully obvious that England would have to import the necessary acetone from countries where huge forests made it easy to produce the chemical in large quantities. As a member of the British Empire, Canada was an ideal choice, and Peuchen managed sprawling lots of timber from which his company produced huge quantities of acetone. Tankers would cross the Atlantic carrying all the acetone that the Mother Country would need.

The Cunard Line's "no-frills" ocean liner *Carpathia* rescued 705 victims of the *Titanic* disaster that occurred more than one hundred years ago.

It was this business opportunity that resulted in the major visiting his business contacts in England, "just in case." Following the meetings, Peuchen booked his return passage on the maiden voyage of the world's newest and most luxurious ocean liner. He planned to be back in his Jarvis Street home shortly after *Titanic* docked in New York on April 17, 1912.

But everything changed at 11:40 on the evening of April 14, 1912, when the giant liner struck an iceberg. Less than three hours later she slipped under the North Atlantic's icy waters.

This Toronto newspaper ad ran in February 1912, two months before the *Titanic* struck an iceberg. In a strange twist, both the ill-fated *Titanic* and the *Carpathia* — the ship that raced to aid *Titanic*'s passengers and crew — appeared in the same advertisement.

But if the major thought his troubles were over when he stepped ashore, boy was he wrong. One of the first things he did when confronted by an eager press was to announce to one and all that the disaster was as a result of (in Peuchen's own words in the *Toronto Globe*) "gross carelessness." He went on to condemn the ship's captain: "[He] knew we were going into an ice field — why would he remain dining in the saloon when such danger was about?"

His criticism of Captain Smith came back to haunt him when it was pointed out that of the hundreds of male passengers who drowned, he was one of very few to survive. Peuchen argued that because of his expertise as a member of Toronto's Royal Canadian Yacht Club he was actually ordered to help with the passengers in Lifeboat #6.

His explanation fell on many deaf ears, however, and for the rest of his life his experience on that terrible night continued to haunt him. Peuchen died in December 1929, and is buried in Mount Pleasant Cemetery in Toronto.

April 18, 2010

The Man Behind Sunnybrook

O ver the years, generations of Torontonians have been the recipients of a variety of parks, large and small, many of which have been donated by citizens eager to enhance the green spaces throughout the city. Their actions have made Toronto what it is today, "a city within a park."

One of the largest of these donations took place in May 1928 when Alice Kilgour, the widow of prominent city businessman, sportsman, and benefactor Joseph Kilgour, presented the city with the deed to the couple's 70.8-hectare (175-acre) Sunnybrook Farm.

Aerial view of Sunnybrook Hospital as it looked not long after it opened as a military hospital in 1948. The intersection at the top left of the image is Bayview Avenue and Blythwood Road.

City of Toronto Archives.

Joseph Kilgour, the landlord of the sprawling Sunnybrook Farm, seen here with his horse Twilight.

Joseph and his brother Robert were in the paper and cardboard manufacturing business. One of their products was the highly popular "snap action" paper bag, the kind that the user was able to open wide with a simple flick of the wrist. It made the boys millionaires.

To honour the family that provided the land for a public park and (later) a hospital, the Leaside town council suggested in 1928 that Bayview Avenue be renamed Kilgour Avenue. The name was never changed, but a small street in the area was recently christened Kilgour Road.

The large Kilgour Brothers factory was located at 21–23 Wellington Street West and was one of the few buildings in the downtown area of the city to have its own sprinkler system, which was supplied with water from two giant storage tanks on the roof. Although the structure suffered minor water and smoke damage during the Great Toronto Fire in April 1904, it was this protection that prevented the conflagration from getting a hold on nearby buildings on the west side of Yonge Street. Had that happened, the acting fire chief was convinced that the fire, though disastrous, would have been much, much worse.

In 1909, Joseph, like many other Toronto men of substance, purchased a large parcel of land out in the county on the east side of the First Concession east of Yonge and just north of Eglinton Avenue. Covering two hundred acres and stretching farther east to today's Leslie Street, it was here that he built a beautiful residence, modern farm buildings, and, being a talented horseman, a collection of well-appointed stables. (Several of the stables were used for years by the Toronto Police Mounted Unit before they moved to the CNE's Horse Palace. They now house a private riding stable.)

Sadly, Joseph Kilgour was only able to enjoy his suburban residence for sixteen years before passing away in early 1925 while on vacation in Florida.

After some deliberation, his widow decided to honour her husband's memory by donating their farm to the citizens of Toronto. And so it was that on May 9, 1928, even though the property was technically outside the city limits of the day, Toronto's inventory of parks grew by 175 acres. One condition she imposed was that the property was to remain a park, forever.

So impressed were civic officials with the Kilgour's donation that they suggested that Bayview Avenue be renamed Kilgour Avenue. For unknown reasons, however, that never happened, but in recent years a small street just south of the new CNIB headquarters was named Kilgour. Better than nothing, I guess.

In 1943, and with a world war raging, officials managing the Kilgour estate approved the construction of a much-needed military hospital on a portion of the park. Today, that hospital has retained part of the Sunnybrook Farm title in its name.

May 9, 2010

Paying Homage to the Temple

In the ongoing race to present the city with the ultimate in condominium towers, a 2010 announcement trumpeted the news that the nation's tallest residential building, a seventy-five-storey, 931-suite skyscraper to be known as the Aura would soon soar to a height of 245-metres (804-feet) at the northwest corner of Yonge and Gerrard. As exciting as that announcement may have been, it was probably no more exciting, in relative terms, than the announcement made in the spring of 1895 by the Independent Order of Foresters that the organization was going to build the city's very first authentic skyscraper. Not only that, but it would also be the tallest building in the entire country, nay the entire British Empire. And befitting its lofty place in the world of architecture, it would be known as the Temple Building.

The idea of creating this million-dollar landmark, one that would dwarf all the other buildings on the city skyline, was presented to the officials of the Independent Order of Foresters (IOF), a member-based insurance organization, by Dr. Oronhyatekha ("Burning Sky"), its popular leader, a full Mohawk chief who was born at Six Nations in 1841. He was also an accomplished medical doctor.

The new IOF building was designed by prominent city architect George Gouinlock, who was also responsible for several of the CNE's older structures, including the Main, now Press Building (1905), the

Horticultural Building (1907), and the Dominion and Provincial, later Arts, Crafts and Hobbies, and now Medieval Times Building (1912).

The view looking north on Bay Street, circa 1900, shows the clock tower of the brand new City Hall in the background and the spectacular (for the day) Temple Building at the corner of Richmond Street.

The Temple Building at the northwest corner of Bay and Richmond streets, circa 1910.

His towering new structure would consist of a massive stone base and thousands and thousands of bricks churned out by the Don Valley Brick Works (located adjacent to the Bayview Extension) all wrapped around a cast-iron skeleton, a building material that was soon to be replaced by structural steel. The structure would soar twelve storeys into the heavens. Canadians had never seen anything like it.

Tenants moved in to the state-of-the-art building (it had electric lighting and two elevators) in 1897. For the next seven decades it was home to a wide variety of companies, although the original IOF offices outgrew the building and in 1954 moved into a new building on Jarvis Street, and then, in Canada's Centennial Year, to a modern new building at the southeast corner of Eglinton Avenue East and Don Mills Road.

By the end of 1970, Toronto's Temple Building had been reduced to rubble.

May 16, 2010

Horsing Around with the Past

While there are numerous pieces of public art, as well as hundreds of monuments and statues to be found in all areas of our city, there are only a couple that feature horses. One of the most obvious is the Steve Stavros Memorial located in Mount Pleasant Cemetery. It may depict the Macedonian king Alexander the Great astride his favourite mount, Bucephalus. I say "may," since I have yet to find specific details about the monument. Therefore, I admit right up front that my description is an assumption and is based on the fact that the eclectic Mr. Stavros, who died in 2006, was a proud Canadian of Macedonia descent and a confirmed lover of race horses. I wonder if I'm correct.

The only other major sculpture that I can think of that features a horse is the King Edward VII statue located just north of the Ontario Legislative Building in the Queen's Park. I call it "the" Queen's Park, since it was named in honour of the reigning monarch of the day, Queen Victoria, by her then-nineteen-year-old son Edward, the Prince of Wales, during his visit to Toronto in 1860. When Victoria died in 1901, Edward ascended the British throne as King Edward VII.

Relatively new to our city, the three-ton monument was originally created in 1919 by the English sculptor Sir Thomas Brock, who was also responsible for the massive Victoria Memorial in front of Buckingham

Palace in London. Brock's tribute to the queen's son (who reigned for a mere nine years compared to his mother's nearly sixty-four years) was originally placed in Delhi, India, but when that country became a sovereign state in 1950 many of the items from the British colonial days were hidden away.

Courtesy of the Honourable Henry N.R. Jackman.

Unveiled in 1969, this statue of King Edward VII is located in Queen's Park, north of the Ontario Legislative Building.

Here are some more horses, although this time they're in the form of mechanical horses under the hoods of these vehicles seen northbound on University Avenue at Richmond Street, circa 1947.

In 1964, the abandoned King Edward VII statue came to the attention of Canada's High Commissioner to India, Roland Michener, who three years later was to become the nation's governor general. He contacted Toronto businessman and philanthropist Henry Jackman and, with funds raised by public donations, it wasn't long before the king and his horse (albeit in pieces) were on their way to Toronto.

Once reassembled, the city's newest landmark was ready for unveiling at an event that took place in 1969. Oh, and just as Roy Rogers had "Trigger," and Gene Autry had "Champion," King Edward had "Kildare," a name that could be the answer to a fascinating game of Toronto trivia.

May 23, 2010

A Royal Trip Around T.O.

The year 1939 was special for our country and for virtually every one of its 11,267,000 citizens. In the spring of that year, King George VI and his consort, Queen Elizabeth, came for a visit. Arriving aboard the Canadian Pacific liner *Empress of Australia* at Quebec City on May 17, the royal couple spent the next month touring the nation from coast to coast, departing Halifax on June 15.

Torontonians were particularly eager to welcome their king and queen. Huge crowds turned out see Their Majesties during their public appearances at Exhibition Park, Riverdale Park, and at the Woodbine Race Track, where they watched the eightieth running of the King's Plate. Thousands more viewed the royal couple and waved from vantage points along the miles of city streets traversed by their maroon McLaughlin Buick touring car during their day-long visit on May 22.

In honour of the royal visit, Toronto's new municipal aerodrome located across the Western Channel at the foot and Bathurst Street and just west of the Hanlan's Point ferry dock and picnic grounds was officially given the title Port George VI Island Airport. However, not long after the couple returned to England, the name was simplified to Toronto Island Airport. After another name change in 1994 it became Toronto City Centre Airport. A further change was recommended in 2009, and it officially became the Billy Bishop Toronto City Airport.

Haven't checked its name lately, but it's quite likely that it's still "Billy's Field."

There's another name in the west end of town that perpetuates memories of that long-ago visit, despite what some of our young citizens may think. Today's modern multi-lane Queen Elizabeth Highway does not recognize the present Queen of Canada (nor do the initials ER along the way stand for Eleanor Roosevelt). The highway does, in fact, honour her mother, the same lady who accompanied the king on that royal visit back in 1939. Of course, provincial officials had to get the queen's approval to so designate the new highway, which, it is reported, she gave with great pleasure.

While today we refer to the entire eighty-six-mile stretch from Highway 427 (on Toronto's western outskirts) to Fort Erie as the QEW, the original Queen Elizabeth Way was only that portion between St. Catharines and Niagara Falls. This stretch (and only this stretch) was so dedicated by Queen Elizabeth on June 7, 1939.

Originally known as the Middle Road, so named because it was located between the Lakeshore Road and the Dundas Highway (#5), the routing of this pioneer thoroughfare would become the right-of-way for the Toronto–Hamilton section of the new Queen Elizabeth Highway. This 1923 photo is from the Ontario Archives.

During their visit to Canada in 1939, King George VI and Queen Elizabeth spent some time in Toronto. On May 22 they visited Woodbine Park (Queen Street East) to watch the eightieth running of the King's Plate. Two weeks later, the queen dedicated the St. Catharines–Niagara Falls section of new Queen Elizabeth Way.

Meanwhile, on the other side of the lake, the new Toronto–Burlington/Hamilton Highway (they hadn't yet decided on its final name) was still being referred to as the New Middle Road Highway.

This highway was merely an upgraded version of the existing Middle Road that had started life as an extension of Toronto's Queen Street and was given the name the Middle Road because it was located midway between the ancient Lake Shore Road and the Dundas Highway.

It wasn't until August 23, 1940, that provincial officials declared the stretch of highway that ran between Toronto and Niagara Falls open. The entire stretch would be known as the Queen Elizabeth Highway. Another year would pass before extensions to the Rainbow Bridge and to Fort Erie opened to traffic.

June 6, 2010

Namesake Is Forever Yonge

Aw nuts! I forgot his birthday again. And now it's too late to send him a card. Actually it's much too late, since he passed away in 1812. And while I haven't yet mentioned this person's name, it's one that virtually every Torontonian, heck every Ontarian, or quite possibly every Canadian, will recognize instantly. He's the man for whom Toronto's main street is named.

Interestingly, Sir George Yonge (his actual birth date was June 17, 1731) never even visited our community. So perhaps one has reason to wonder how his name came to be attached to one of the nation's best-known streets, the very same street that was recognized for a time by the Guinness people as the world's longest (changes to the provincial highway system made in 1998 by the Mike Harris government put an end to that claim to fame).

The real reason for Yonge Street being so named has more to do with the province's first lieutenant governor, John Graves Simcoe, than anything else. And here's why. Soon after Simcoe's arrival from England in 1792 to begin his tenure, he started to change many of the existing place names because, as he often stated, their sounds were "foreign to his ears." Thus Cataraqui became Kings Town (Kingston), Niagara became the New Ark (Newark, now Niagara-on-the-Lake), and the most foreign of all, Toronto, became York (to honour King George III's second eldest son, Frederick, the Duke of ... you guessed it, York!

Looking south on Yonge Street from just south of the dusty Lawrence Avenue inter-section, circa 1905. Note the tracks of the Toronto and York Radial Railway, a sort of early GO Transit operation that carried people and freight to and from the city on high-speed electric streetcars.

Just days before the new Yonge subway was to open, a crowd waits to board a north-bound Yonge streetcar at the Richmond Street intersection, March 28, 1954.

And when it came time to give a name to the new path his Rangers were cutting through the forested hinterland north of the York town site, Simcoe remembered his neighbour back in Devon, a man who had also been a colleague of his in the British House of Parliament.

Sir George Yonge, 5th Baronet, was born in a little Devon town called Colyton and he was destined to serve as the country's Secretary at War (1782–1794), Master of the Mint (1794–1799), and the governor of the Cape Colony (1799–1801).

As important as these positions were, it's more likely that Simcoe selected his friend's name because of Yonge's fascination with and expertise in the art of Roman road-building.

What better tribute than to name the pioneer road Yonge Street.

June 20, 2010

Sir George Yonge (1731–1812), in whose honour Toronto's main street is named.

Royal Twist to Street Name

There is still much interest in this country today in the affairs of the British Royal Family, so I thought it only fitting to present my readers with a column with a "royal" twist. That twist has to do with the name of one of Toronto's most interesting streets and one that bears the name of our present queen's (Elizabeth II) great-great-grandmother.

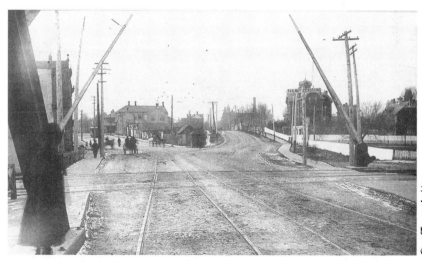

Queen Street, looking west toward the split with King Street, just west of the Don River. Note the dangerous level railway crossing, which disappeared when the present bridge was built in 1911. This view is circa 1900.

Looking west along Queen Street from the bridge over the Don River, 1948.

A similar view today.

Soon after the community we now know as Toronto was established by Lieutenant Governor John Simcoe in 1793, his land surveyors created a map of the area on which an east–west "base line" was delineated. Starting at this important geographical element and moving northward, additional east–west streets were added to the map, with each of these being exactly one hundred chains apart (a chain being a surveyor's measuring device, with one chain equal to sixty-six feet). Mathematically, this one-hundred-chain distance translates into 6,600 feet, or one and a quarter miles. These streets, known as concession roads in the beginning, would eventually become the major east–west crossroads we now know as Bloor, St. Clair, Eglinton, Lawrence, York Mills/Wilson, Sheppard, Finch, and Steeles.

The original "base line," which ran across the bottom of the grid, eventually took on the descriptive name Lot Street because it formed the southern boundary of the one-hundred-acre parcels of land (or lots) that were awarded to the settlement's privileged newcomers. These lots were a kind of reward for giving up the amenities of the province's established communities, such as Kings Town (Kingston) or Newark (Niagara-on-the-Lake) for a life in the undeveloped hinterland around York.

It wasn't until after Alexandrina Victoria (the granddaughter of King George III, after whom our King Street is named) ascended to the throne of the United Kingdom in 1837 that her loyal subjects here in Toronto changed the name of Lot Street to Queen Street to honour their new monarch.

July 4, 2010

Daring Young Man over T.O.

In this day and age, people seldom look skyward when an airplane flies overhead. But that certainly wasn't the case in 1910, for on July 13 of that year local aviation history was made.

Courtesy of Michael deLesseps (Jacques' grandson).

Count Jacques deLesseps, who became the first person to pilot an aircraft over the city of Toronto.

It all started a few days earlier as the first Toronto Aviation Meet got underway on July 8. Sponsored in part by the Ontario Motor League (now the CAA), daily admission to the nine-day show was $1 for adults and 65¢ for children. The event was held at the Trethewey Model Farm northwest of the city near the town of Weston and was advertised to run through July 16 (but never on a Sunday in good old Toronto). Several well-known aviators were invited to attend and demonstrate their newest "flying machines."

Among the guests was French aviator Count Jacques deLesseps, who arrived at the temporary

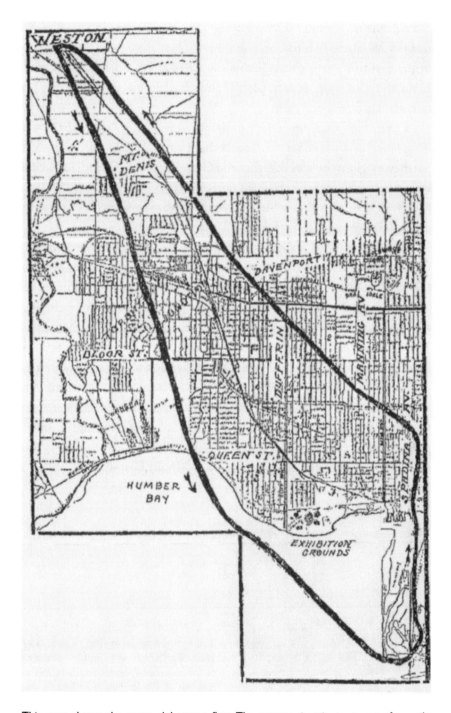

This map shows the route deLesseps flew. The twenty-six-minute, twenty-four-mile jaunt provided many Torontonians with their first glimpse of an airplane.

airfield on the opening day following his participation at a similar air meet in Montreal that had only recently ended. The count, who was one of the first to fly an airplane across the English Channel, brought with him two of his monoplanes, both Bleriot models, one of which was his famous "La Scarabee."

Over the next few days, aviators and their "state-of-the-art aeroplanes" performed for the crowds that had made their way out to Mr. Trethewey's farm by way of either the Grand Trunk or Canadian Pacific Railways, each of which provided transportation ("at close intervals") to and from the city's Union Station, which at that time was located west of York Street at the foot of today's University Avenue.

As entertaining as these short hops around the field were, it was Count Jacques deLesseps who decided to add a little something extra to the mix. So, early on the evening of July 13, he took to the cool night air as he had done on every day of the meet, but instead of simply circling the farm field, the count pointed La Scarabee's nose south toward Humber Bay. A few minutes later he turned the craft eastward toward Hanlan's Point, swooping low over the Lakeside Home for Children (a summer retreat for the young patients of the Hospital for Sick Children then located on the island). Turning northward, his monoplane then followed Spadina Avenue before banking slightly over the College Street intersection. The count then set his sights on the Davenport hill on Dufferin Street and the community of Mount Dennis.

The model farm of mining expert G.W. Trethewey, which was located southeast of the town of Weston, was selected as the site of the Toronto Air Meet. It was from this grass field that deLesseps took off before making his historic flight over Toronto on July 13, 1910.

Arriving back at the Trethewey farm a full twenty-six minutes after he departed, the count's historic flight had covered an estimated twenty-four miles at heights reaching up to four thousand feet. And what made the flight even more memorable was the fact that it was the first time the vast majority of Torontonians had ever seen an airplane. In fact, in their bewilderment, many telephoned the city newspapers or the local police station in an attempt to find out what they had witnessed in the skies over their city.

As we now know, the daring feat performed by Count Jacques deLessep's in his La Scarabee monoplane on that day in 1910 was the first flight of an airplane over the city of Toronto.

July 11, 2010

Ritzy Hotel Shot for the Green

L ocated at the northwest corner of Bloor Street West and Royal York Road is a former branch of the Royal Bank of Canada. Over the entrance to what is now a coffee shop, you will find a splendid likeness of the old City of Toronto coat-of-arms.

It's quiz time! What does the Royal York Hotel have to do with the name of a street in the west end of Toronto? Give up? Read on.

This June 1927 sketch of the proposed Royal York Hotel appeared at about the same time its owner, the CPR, was contemplating building a suburban golf course that would be available exclusively to its guests.

When the Canadian Pacific Railway announced it was going to build a mammoth new hotel on Front Street in downtown Toronto, company officials were looking at various ways to make the hotel special and to draw customers away from the existing city hotels, especially the venerable King Edward.

The first thing they did was to ensure that access to and from the city's new (but still unopened) Union Station, which had been built across the street from the hotel, was as easy as possible. So in order to eliminate the need to negotiate the vehicular and streetcar traffic on busy Front Street, a pedestrian tunnel was built connecting the two buildings. Little did those officials know that this short underground passage would be a precursor of the twenty-eight kilometres of underground walkways that make up today's sprawling PATH network.

Another amenity that the new hotel would offer its guests was a "pay as you play membership" in an eighteen-hole golf course that the CPR planned to develop on land owned by the Toronto Land Corporation in the suburban Township of Etobicoke. This latter company, under the direction of Robert Home Smith, had been responsible for the construction of dozens of beautiful homes that surrounded the nearby Old Mill, a structure that Home Smith himself had opened in 1914 as a kind of recreation centre for the prestigious Humber Valley Surveys community he was developing adjacent to the Humber River.

Work on the new $75,000 course, which was designed by Toronto-born and world-renowned golf course architect Stanley Thompson, began in the fall of 1928. A little more than a year later, Canada's best-known golfer, George S. Lyon, laid the cornerstone of the new $150,000 clubhouse, which featured a large dining room and ten bedrooms.

Incidentally, George Lyon remains the only person to have won a gold medal in golf at the Summer Olympics. He did so by defeating

Royal York Road was originally known as Church Street.

seventy-seven other golfers during the 1904 edition of the games. Then, for some reason, golf was removed from contention in all future Olympic Games. It is scheduled to be re-introduced as an event in the 2016 Olympics to be held in Rio de Janeiro.

When the golf course opened in May 1930, it was officially known as the Royal York Hotel Golf Club, though it operated as simply the Royal York Golf Club.

A little piece of old Toronto still exists in Etobicoke.

It wasn't long before the name of one of the narrow roads leading north to the new course from the Lake Shore Road was changed from the original Church Street to Royal York Road.

Early in 1946, the CPR divested itself of the Etobicoke property, returning it to the original landowner, the Toronto Land Corporation. At the same time it was agreed that the name of the club would be changed, and after some discussion the membership decided on St. George's Golf and Country Club. Many prestigious tournaments have been held at the course over the years, including the 2010 Canadian Open.

July 18, 2010

Evolution of Transportation

As the TTC mulls over various ways to make fare payment easier and more cost-effective, let's look back more than a century to a time when the commission's predecessor introduced another interesting feature that was destined, for a time at least, to make taking public transportation more convenient.

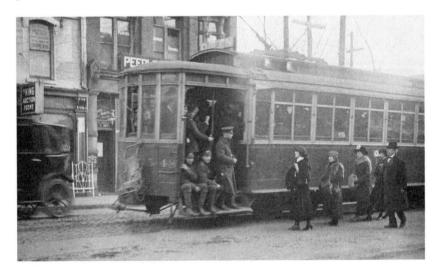

Queen Street east of Spadina Avenue, circa 1918. Note the baby carriage hanging from a hook at the back of the streetcar. Note also the soldiers who have only recently returned from the Great War.

The company that introduced the "baby carriage hook" that was affixed on the back of its streetcars was the privately owned Toronto Railway Company (TRC). It took over the operation of the city's public transportation requirements on September 1, 1891. It did so soon after the termination of a similar monopoly that had been the responsibility of another private operator, the Toronto Street Railway (TSR). The TSR's franchise began in 1861 and, like that of its successor, was meant to run for thirty years. However, for a variety of reasons the Street Railway Company's tenure ended in mid-May of its final year. And that's when the city became the operator. However, a lack of expertise in providing what Torontonians felt was an acceptable service forced the city fathers to get out of the business. On September 1, 1891, the Toronto Railway Company took over.

Courtesy of the TTC/Mike de Toma.

While the baby carriage hooks may have disappeared, another convenience feature, the bicycle rack, can be found on hundreds of Toronto's city buses.

More a safety feature than a convenience feature, "fenders" (more popularly known back in the olden days as cowcatchers) were installed in the 1890s on Toronto Railway streetcars. The devices were instrumental in preventing numerous pedestrian injuries, or, more importantly, fatalities.

One of the problems faced by Torontonians with this new service was the fact that it didn't extend out into the suburban areas of the fast-growing city. And while the city tried to get the TRC to lay track into the more sparsely settled suburban areas, the company staunchly refused after figuring that the cost to do so far outweighed any profits they could realize. Access to the city got so bad that the city's legal officials took the matter to the highest courts in England, only to have the city's request that the street railway company be ordered to expand its system rejected. The court agreed that the company only had to provide service within the city boundaries as they had stood when the original agreement was signed in 1891.

As a result, riders living in the suburbs continued to have a long walk to the nearest streetcar line. Many of those customers were women with babies in carriages, and the streetcar company at least went to the expense of affixing steel hooks to the back of the cars, which allowed the women to hang the carriages outside the vehicles.

When the new municipally owned TTC took over in the fall of 1921 the area of the city being served increased dramatically. For this reason, in addition to the safety concerns, the convenience of hanging a baby carriage on the back of a streetcar became just a memory.

To learn more about the history of Toronto streetcars and those of several other Ontario communities (and even to ride them), why not spend a day at the Halton County Radial Railway Museum. This entertaining family attraction is located on the Guelph Line, ten miles north of Highway 401 (Exit 312). More details can be found on the museum's website, *www.hcry.org*, or they can be contacted by phone at 519-856-9802.

July 25, 2010

Long Track to Union Station's Opening

It was on Saturday, August 6, 1927 that Toronto's magnificent new Union Station was officially opened by Edward, Prince of Wales. It was an unusual event in that, other than someone in the royal party eyeballing the new building and making the observation that "here in Canada you build your railway stations like we build cathedrals back home," the whole thing took but a few minutes.

In 1958, the same people who gave Canada the CF-100 jet fighter and the revolutionary Jetliner passenger plane and Arrow supersonic interceptor suggested they could develop a high-speed monorail from Malton Airport to downtown Toronto.

A monorail was also proposed as an alternate to a regular subway under Bloor Street. This sketch shows the corner of Bay and Bloor as it might have been. The first section of the Bloor-Danforth subway opened underground at this corner in 1966.

Such minimal observance must have been anti-climactic for all those involved in the station's construction. After all, almost two decades had gone by since the day back in 1905 that the federal government ordered a new terminal for Toronto be erected "without delay." In addition, the station wasn't even completely ready for ordinary rail passengers.

In fact, with the abbreviated formalities concluded (the prince would return to the city at the end of the month, along with his brother Prince George, to dedicate the new eastern entrance at the CNE) the station doors were quickly closed and did not reopen for another three days. Disappointed passengers were forced to continue using the "ancient" 1872-era Union Station some distance to the west.

Even when the new facility finally opened to the general public on August 11, it was still not capable of functioning as it had been designed. The main drawback was the location of the tracks. From the very beginning, Toronto's new station was to be of the "through" design and not a "terminal" station — one where trains ended their journeys.

In order to make Toronto's new facility a through station, it would be necessary to allow pedestrian and vehicle traffic to use the adjacent and very busy north–south streets — Yonge, Bay and York — unimpeded. This required that the tracks entering and leaving the station be elevated well above those streets on a massive viaduct. Construction of that viaduct was a very expensive proposition. And then there was the matter of who would pay for it. Years went by before a deal was struck. And then it took more time to actually build the viaduct.

Finally, on January 21, 1930 (a quarter-century after the government ordered the station built), trains began using the elevated entrance to Union Station. Many years later it was decided that a brand new transportation facility was needed. This would necessitate the demolition of Union Station. A public outcry soon changed that plan, and today the station is in the midst of getting a $640-million upgrade.

While rail travel remains a popular way of getting from here to there, there was an attempt back in the mid-1950s to interest the city fathers in a variation of the regular twin-track railway — the monorail. One suggestion was that part of the proposed Bloor-Danforth subway be built as a monorail, as promoted by a company out of Houston, Texas. That plan was laughed out of the council chamber.

Even more interesting was a 1958 proposal to connect the city's main airport, then known as Malton Airport (after the small community adjacent to it), with the downtown via a high-speed monorail, utilizing the existing CN rail corridor. It was also suggested that all the necessary technology could be developed by the people at Avro Canada, who at the time were working on the Arrow jet interceptor. While building hundreds of this revolutionary new aircraft for the RCAF would keep the factory busy, there was enough skilled Avro staff to start a whole new monorail industry.

But in the end, no Arrow and no monorail.

August 8, 2010

When T.O. Got Wired

It was August 15, 1892, that Toronto's civic leaders climbed aboard streetcar no. 270 in front of the city hall located at the southwest corner of Front and Jarvis and headed off into history. The occasion was the introduction of electric streetcar service, a modern new way of travel that within a couple of years would replace the traditional horse-drawn vehicles that had carried thousands and thousands of Torontonians around since 1861.

The plan to convert the city system from real horsepower to the electric kind was included as one of the details in the thirty-year monopoly awarded to the Toronto Railway Company by the city in 1891. What wasn't set out was just what form the new system would take. The recent discovery of electricity and its "magic power" that was able to replace "man" power and, in the case of transportation, "horse" power, had resulted in numerous experiments being undertaken across the globe.

As for street railway equipment, a young fellow by the name of Thomas Edison was absolutely convinced that huge storage batteries would be perfect to power the new electric streetcars. These onboard batteries would eliminate the need for overhead wires. However, just as today, the use of batteries to provide sufficient motive power for extended periods of time was something that even the great Edison soon found impractical. Before long, he turned all his efforts to the science of light and sound.

A committee to examine the different methods of transportations that could be used here in our city was set up by Mayor R.J. Fleming. In the spring of 1892, its members were off on a fact-finding mission, visiting several large American cities that were also studying how best to implement a new electric streetcar service.

In addition to the storage battery car idea (that given the technology of the day turned out to be a waste of time), another method that looked promising was the placement of an electrically charged wire in a slot between the tracks. A metal finger sticking down under the car would ride along the wire and conduct the electricity to the car's controller and motor. It was an interesting concept, but then someone pointed out that leaves, dirt, snow, and ice (all prevalent in Toronto) could easily plug the slot.

Finally, at a special meeting of the Toronto City Council on May 13, 1892, it was agreed, though not unanimously, that a third method, the overhead wire and trolley pole (as pioneered seven years earlier at the Toronto Industrial Exhibition, now the CNE) would be the best system for Toronto.

Toronto's first electric streetcar went into operation on August 15, 1892. This 1894 view is of a similar vehicle (#216), seen here travelling eastbound on Queen Street in front of the Gladstone Hotel. In the background is the awkward Dufferin, Queen, and Gladstone intersection that recently underwent major realignment.

Within days, poles and wire were being strung and steel rails were being welded to create the necessary return circuit. The company had several electric vehicles ready to test the system, and on August 10 a special trial run was carried out. All went well that day, allowing the company president to proudly announce that the first revenue operation would take place the following Monday, August 15.

With civic officials and a few cautious but curious members of the public onboard (and hundreds more lining the streets), the first electric car headed north on Church Street. When it reached Bloor, it slowly turned the corner and headed east to Sherbourne, where it turned north, crossed the bridge over the Rosedale Ravine, and came to the end of the line in a new loop just across the Sherbourne Street bridge. The obligatory speeches and toasts to the city and the company, as well as to anything or anybody they could think of, were given before lunch was served. Toronto was an electric streetcar city. And you know what? It still is.

August 15, 2010

Courtesy of the TTC/Bombardier.

Though the design has yet to be finalized, this is a close approximation of what Toronto's new low-floor light-rail streetcar, the *Bombardier Legacy* model, will look like.

Agriculture Fair Sprouts the Ex

O ur good old CNE's roots go back to the mid-1840s. The "Ex" originally began as a peripatetic agricultural fair — meaning one that wandered each year to a different town or city somewhere in the province. The event was actually the child of the Provincial Agricultural Association and Board of Agriculture for Canada West (renamed Ontario after the creation of the Dominion of Canada on July 1, 1867) and, as the organizing committee's name suggests, the fair's emphasis was on all things agricultural. By 1878 the event had become so popular that many believed that, rather than making attendees wander all over the province, it should be held each year in one location. With Toronto being both the provincial capital and the most important city in the nation at the time, it was thought that this was where it should be held. For various political reasons the founding organization didn't feel the same way, and it ordered that the 1879 edition of the fair be held in Ottawa.

"Hold it wherever you like," was the Toronto contingent's reply. "We'll hold our own right here." And with that decision, the Toronto Industrial Exhibition was born, with the first edition of this new Toronto attraction being held during the first three weeks of September 1879 on the Garrison Common (a large piece of waterfront property that incorporated much of today's Exhibition Place).

Courtesy of CNE Archives.

Built during the depths of the Second World, CNR locomotive 6213 was retired from service in 1959. The following year it was moved and put on display adjacent to the Marine Museum in Exhibition Place where for the next nearly half-century it was admired and photographed by thousands.

Courtesy of Lance Gleich.

Locomotive 6213 now has a new and far more appropriate home. It is the centrepiece of the Toronto Railway Heritage Centre located at the John Street Roundhouse building at the base of the CN Tower.

As exemplified by the title of the new Toronto fair, agriculture, while still important to the province's economy, was being overtaken by the display of Canadian manufactured items.

Some of the things on display at what would officially be renamed the Canadian National Exhibition in 1912 included tractors (from the Massey Manufacturing factory next door to the fairgrounds), a variety of steam engines, mammoth water pumps, and electric lighting equipment. And it wasn't long before several examples of the newest marvel of the age, the horseless carriage, were drawing crowds with the locally-built Russell automobile frequently stealing the show. Incidentally, this innovative vehicle was created by the forerunner of the CCM Company (better known in later years for its hockey equipment) and was built in a factory on Weston Road. It was named in honour of Tommy Russell, CCM's long-time company president, who also served as CNE president.

While on the subject of transportation, visitors to the fair will now notice that CNR's retired 6213 Northern-type locomotive and tender are no longer on display in behind the midway rides and concession booths on the south side of the grounds. In fact, it was just a few weeks before the 2009 fair that 6213 was moved to its new and much more appropriate (and certainly more visible) home in the 1929 John Street Roundhouse located at the Canadian Railway Heritage Centre near the base of the CN Tower. Here, along with a large number of other railway-related artifacts (including a miniature railway and the restored 120-foot-long turntable), visitors are transported back in our nation's history to a time when the railway was king.

To learn more about this attraction, which is run by a team of dedicated volunteers, visit *www.trha.ca*.

August 22, 2010

Good, Plane Fun at the Ex

While the CNE is well-known for its midway rides, talented street performers, and the always-busy Food Building, I don't think anyone would disagree that the air show continues to be the most exciting attraction at each year's fair. This event attracts thousands to the Ex each year, with lots of time left over to take in the other sights and sounds in and around our wonderful city.

Known officially as the Canadian International Air Show since its inception as a two-day aerial event during the 1956 CNE, today's CIAS is quite literally the successor to the very first air show ever witnessed by an astounded Canadian public.

That history-making show was held on the Lake Ontario shoreline several miles east of today's CNE waterfront. Located between today's MacLean and Leuty Avenues, Scarboro Beach Park consisted of a sprawling picnic ground, several thrilling rides, various games of chance, and a large sports field. In many ways it was in direct competition with the Exhibition from the year it opened in 1907 until it closed in 1925.

Near the end of the 1909 season, the management of Scarboro Beach was able to sign a deal with pioneer American aviator Charles Willard. For a certain amount of money (the papers of the day didn't record the exact amount), Willard would take off from the park's shoreline and fly a loop out over the lake. In doing so he would present to a thunderstruck public (who had paid a small fee to witness the event) the country's first public "air show." Unfortunately, Willard's first attempt on September 2 was less than a success, with his "Golden Flyer" travelling only thirty feet before plummeting from a height of twenty feet into the cold lake. It took a few days to make repairs to his craft and on September 7 he tried again. This time he was in the air a full five minutes and travelled nearly two miles out over the lake. This historic flight was followed by a near-perfect landing on the park's sandy beach.

In hindsight, the young aviator should have called it quits then and there and gone back to the States. However, in addition to being an aviator, Willard was a showman, and to give the crowd just one more thrill he would try again on the 10th. Unfortunately, just thirteen seconds into that flight both Willard and his Golden Flyer were back in the water. Oh well, one successful flight out of three wasn't all that bad, I guess. Besides, that one historic flight on the 7th meant that the park's owners could lay claim to it being the site of Canada's first public air show.

A few years later, with the First World War raging in Europe, it was the CNE's turn to host a series of mini air shows, and in doing so helped draw the fairgoer's attention to the fact that airplanes had now become machines of war.

The feature performer, and in fact the only performer in Canada's very first air show, was American aviator Charles Willard piloting his Curtiss "Golden Flyer." The event was held in early September 1909 at Toronto's Scarboro Beach Park.

Once hostilities were over, each successive fair presented some form of aerial demonstration program. Then, with the approach of the 1939 Exhibition, it was obvious that the world would soon be at war again. In an effort to bolster the war effort, CNE management decided to feature, in addition to static military ground displays, a full program of British and Canadian-built warplanes buzzing over the fairgrounds.

A Royal Air Force Vulcan "V-bomber" makes a low-level pass over the CNE Bandshell in 1966. The Vulcan's first visit to the CNE air show was in 1958; its final fly-by was in 1983.

In early 1942 the Exhibition grounds were turned over to the Canadian forces, and for obvious reasons there was no annual fair or air show for the next five years.

Following the return of peace in 1945 (but with the CNE grounds not cleared and available until 1947), an air show was held in 1946 at the de Havilland aircraft factory airfield in North York Township. The same site was chosen for the 1947 show, and the following year Malton Airport was selected to host the event.

The 1949 show returned to the annual CNE with special presentations by the RCAF's revolutionary Vampire jets thrilling noontime crowds. These shows continued through 1955, with the most modern aircraft of the day participating.

The year 1956 saw the premier edition of the Canadian International Air Show, an event that continues to present the world's fastest and most interesting airplanes to large crowds of spectators.

September 5, 2010

Toronto's "New" City Hall Turns 45

When is something that's described as *new* not really new? When it's Toronto's "new" city hall. That's because, even though it's referred to locally as "New City Hall," the building actually just turned 45 years old in 2010. The descriptive preface was added about the time the city's new municipal headquarters opened on September 13, 1965, just across Bay Street from the city hall that had served Toronto since September 18, 1899.

The idea of a brand new facility to take over from what was being described as an "ancient pile of bricks" had been promoted for years. However, it wasn't until Nathan Phillips took over as mayor in 1955 that it looked as if anything would actually happen. The mayor decided to ask the voters if they would approve the construction of a new municipal building at a cost of $18 million. The response was an unequivocal "No!"

Interestingly, one of the designs that was submitted and would have been the city's new municipal building had the project been approved by the electorate was subsequently modified and now stands as the former Imperial Oil Building (and soon to be condominium) on the south side of St. Clair Avenue just west of Yonge Street. (For more on this building, see page 98, City Hall that Might've Been.)

Nothing daunted Mayor Phillips, who tried again, and this time city council approved an "open" competition, something that irked the local architectural community. Nonetheless, the response was amazing, with 520 different concepts submitted from forty-two different countries. A blue-ribbon team of judges began inspecting the submissions, and on September 26, 1958, the city announced the winner, one submitted by Finnish architect Viljo Revell. So revolutionary was his concept (especially for a still somewhat boring city like Toronto) that two of the judges submitted dissenting reports. Nevertheless, it was agreed that Revell's idea was "distinct, dramatic and would set it aside from the office buildings in the area."

Not only were two of the judges unmoved by the choice, many Torontonians were outright uncomplimentary, with some calling it "Nate's clam shell." Nevertheless, the mayor was ecstatic, and after months of preliminary work the first sod was turned on November 7, 1961.

Toronto's new city hall was officially opened by Canada's governor general of the day, Georges Vanier. Unfortunately, Viljo Revell passed away just ten months before the opening.

The ruins of the old Casino Theatre that stood on the south side of Toronto's Queen Street frame Finnish architect Viljo Revell's new city hall.

There's an interesting sideline to the new city hall project. Throughout the nearly four years of construction, city officials fretted over the look of the row of nondescript (and in many cases downright seedy) buildings lining the south side of Queen Street opposite their new $31-million "jewel." The city finally expropriated the properties and, despite a suggestion that the land remain a park, calls for redevelopment were announced. Only three replies were received, one of which was rejected because of financial problems. That left just two.

It began to look as if the office building/hotel project (the hotel would be called the Hotel Toronto) backed by American multi-millionaire Conrad Hilton would win out. But again there was a problem with financing, which resulted in City Council rejecting the plan. In the summer of 1968, the redevelopment of the site was awarded to the Four Seasons-Sheraton group led by Max and Isadore Sharp, whose 125-room Four Seasons motor hotel had opened on Jarvis Street in 1961.

The group's new hotel/shopping concourse project, now known as the Sheraton Centre, opened in the fall of 1972.

September 12, 2010

Inquisitive members of the public examine a model of Toronto's new city hall soon after the design was announced on September 26, 1958.

Next TTC Stop, "Little Norway"

As many of my readers know, throughout the warm weather months I host tours of downtown Toronto aboard one the TTC's two remaining 1950s-era PCC Streamliner streetcars. (By the way, I only wish Mayor Rob Ford would come for a ride and see the smiles on the faces of citizens and tourists alike as we glide by on one of these icons from Toronto's past. He seems to forget Toronto is and will always be a streetcar city, and that many of its citizens are very proud of our streetcar heritage.)

To continue, one of the things that makes conducting these tours so gratifying is when someone in the group remarks that they remembered a building, a park, or perhaps a movie house from their past, something they had forgotten all about it until I mentioned it at some point during the tour. Suddenly the memories come flooding back and you can hear the chatter throughout the streetcar.

Take, for instance, what happened on a tour with a group from Barrie a couple of years ago. As we turned south on Bathurst Street off Fleet, I mentioned as we approached Queen's Quay that just off to the right of the car was the site of what was once known as "Little Norway." That statement certainly brought back a flood of memories for one gentleman, who was familiar with the place because he had served with a Norwegian airman during the Second World War, and one of the ladies on the car told the entire group that she and her friend would often visit

Little Norway on a Sunday afternoon and invite a couple of the young pilots to her parent's house for a real home-cooked meal.

So just what was Little Norway anyway? And what did it have to do with Norway? And why was it located at the foot of Bathurst Street?

Well, here's the story. When Norway was overrun by Nazi Germany in April 1940, the Norwegian government went into exile in England. They quickly decided to relocate the aviators and mechanics of the Royal Norwegian Air Force (who had also escaped) to a location somewhere in North America where they could continue training with every intention of getting back in the war and helping to defeat the invaders. The site that was selected was a piece of barren land that had been reclaimed by the Toronto Harbour Commission. It was located at the foot of Bathurst Street, in behind the old Maple Leaf Stadium (the home since 1926 of the popular Toronto Maple Leaf baseball team). A number of wooden buildings that would be used as barracks, school rooms, dining facilities, etc. were quickly constructed on the mainland side, while the recently opened airport just across the Western Channel, and accessible by a rope ferry, would serve as the airfield.

Aerial view of Toronto's "Little Norway," circa 1941.

Courtesy of Baldur Sveinsson.

Northrop N-3PB, similar to the aircraft that crashed in Toronto Harbour after clipping the top of the Toronto Island ferry *Sam McBride*.

Officially opened in November 1940, the military camp quickly became known as Little Norway. After a while, however, it was decided that the site was too small, and in May 1942 a new, much larger site opened in Muskoka. For a time afterward, Toronto's Little Norway was home to an RCAF facility before it was converted to much-needed wartime housing. After the war, a close-knit community grew at the foot of Bathurst Street.

An interesting but sad event occurred on June 20, 1941, when a training mission flown by two members of the Royal Norwegian Air Force stationed at Little Norway attempted to take off from Toronto Harbour. For reasons never fully identified, their float-equipped Northrop N-3PB patrol bomber clipped the top of the Island ferry *Sam McBride*, flipped over, and crashed into the bay, killing both crew members. Many witnesses said that had the pilot not taken evasive action at the last second, the ferry boat would have been hit, resulting in a much more serious outcome.

In 1976, the former camp was remembered during a special ceremony in which a plaque and a huge three-thousand-pound boulder brought to Toronto from Norway were unveiled by Norwegian Crown Prince Harald. In 1987, King Olav V dedicated the site we know today as Little Norway Park.

September 19, 2010

Waterfront Gem Still Sparkles

In 2010, to celebrate the restored Toronto Island ferry *Trillium*'s one hundredth anniversary (the vessel was launched at the Polson Iron Works at the foot of Sherbourne Street in 1910) the city offered a series of very popular public cruises of Toronto Bay on each of the five Fridays in July. It was from a vantage point out in the bay that those onboard could get a good look at the construction activities that are changing the look of the waterfront, especially the stretch along Queen's Quay from Yonge Street east to Parliament.

While all this work goes on and old structures disappear and new ones take their place there's one constant that reminds us that the redevelopment of the city's waterfront is not new. That constant is the handsome Toronto Harbour Commission Building on Harbour Street, just west of Bay. Designed by Toronto architect Alfred Chapman (Princes' Gates, Sunnyside Bathing Pavilion, Palais Royale) and built at a cost of $247,000, the building opened in 1918 on the water's edge as the seven-year-old commission's headquarters. The site was selected to demonstrate the commissioners' faith in the future of Toronto and its waterfront.

It was in this building that plans for a totally new Toronto waterfront stretching from the Humber River in the west to the border with the Township of Scarborough several miles to the east were developed. As the accompanying photos show, the old building has seen enormous changes to our waterfront over the years, with more to come.

September 26, 2010

A captured German submarine on its way to a museum in Chicago is moored in front of the new Toronto Harbour Commission Building, July 1919.

Toronto's new waterfront takes shape in front of the THC Building, circa 1921.

The handsome Toronto Harbour Commission Building today.

Brave Firemen of Yesteryear

L ate in the afternoon of September 24, 2010, fire erupted and rav-aged a twenty-fourth-floor apartment at 200 Wellesley Street East. Responding to the six-alarm blaze were more than one hundred firefighters and nearly thirty pieces of firefighting equipment. And even while these brave men and women fought the stubborn blaze, little did officials realize just how badly the lives of hundreds of the building's residents would be affected. It would be a week before the first of the affected tenants could return home.

Like all great cities, the history of fire protection and firefighting makes for fascinating reading. In the earliest days of our community, when we were still known as the Town of York and downtown was located in an around today's King and Jarvis intersection, destruction by fire was pretty much an accepted fact of life.

Even when fires erupted during the time York was occupied by American forces during the War of 1812, there was no organized effort to extinguish them. Several prominent structures, including the parliament buildings on the waterfront near the foot of today's Parliament Street (thus the street name) fell victim.

Another seven years would pass before officials came up with any rules to help prevent fires getting out of control and burning down the whole darn town. The first of those rules mandated that two buckets be

Toronto received its first motorized piece of fire apparatus in October 18, 1911.

Outside the city boundaries, the various suburban communities relied on volunteer fire fighters such as these fellows, who served the Town of North Toronto. This community joined the City of Toronto in 1912.

positioned in a conspicuous place near the front door of every building in town. In the event of fire, citizens were expected to form a line between the fire and the bay or the nearest water-filled cistern and pass buckets of water that would (hopefully) douse the flames. In case of a chimney fire, a wooden ladder was nearby to afford access to the roof.

Pictured is one of our community's first pieces of firefighting equipment, which was acquired in the early 1830s. It was hauled by volunteers.

The first major step in providing the citizens with dependable fire protection was instituted in 1826 with the creation of a volunteer (unpaid) fire department. The volunteers served the citizens well, but as the city grew it became obvious a permanent force was necessary. A new city department, the one we know today as Toronto Fire Services, was authorized by city council in 1874. It consisted of fifty officers and men (today's operations staff numbers nearly 2,700) and worked with a budget of $39,916 (2009 net operating budget $361 million).

Up until 1890, the department used horses provided under contract with livery stables to propel its various pieces of fire apparatus through the city streets. It was in that year that the city purchased its first "fleet" of twenty-eight horses for a total cost of $4,630.

Twenty-one years later the department took delivery of its first motorized vehicle, a Seagrave chemical-hose combination engine purchased for $7,850. It was assigned to Fire Station No. 8 at the southwest corner of College and Bellevue.

The modernization of the department's fire apparatus continued, ultimately resulting in the retiring of its last two horses, Mickey and Prince, in April of 1931. These two "fire warriors" had served the city for a total of twenty-nine years, and during that time had answered more than 2,500 alarm calls. Both were retired to a farm in Whitby.

October 10, 2010

City Hall that Might've Been

A s I've mentioned in previous columns, my first full-time job following graduation from Ryerson Polytechnical Institute was with the Ontario Water Resources Commission (that years later would become part of what is known today as the Ontario Ministry of the Environment). My office was at the corner of Avenue Road and St. Clair Avenue West, and often at lunch hour several of my co-workers and I would make the trek over to Yonge Street. In doing so we would walk past the imposing Imperial Oil Building at 111 St. Clair.

One day while scanning an old newspaper (which I did on my own time, never on the OWRC's nickel) I came across an article dated November 17, 1955. It showed a proposal (seen here) that had been put forward by a consortium of prominent Canadian architectural firms (Marani and Morris, Mathers and Haldenby, and Shore and Moffat) in response to a comment made by city alderman Nathan Phillips during his successful campaign to be elected mayor for the year 1955.

As part of his campaign, Phillips had remarked several times that the city definitely needed a new city hall to replace "that ancient pile of stone" at the top of Bay Street. In late 1955, with nearly a full year as Chief Magistrate under his belt (and with municipal elections an annual event), Mayor Phillips made another pitch for a new city hall, and to that end was convincing enough in his arguments before his city council members to get the question "should Toronto build a new city hall at an estimated cost of $18 million" placed on the December 5, 1955, ballot.

Here it should be pointed out that the "proposed" design for a new city hall that appeared in the November 17, 1955, newspaper article was not sanctioned by the mayor but rather simply a suggestion put forward by the consortium involved.

Unfortunately for Mayor Phillips, the electorate rejected the idea of a new city hall, with 32,564 voters against and only 28,449 agreeing that a new building was needed. Nothing daunted the mayor, however, and he had the project cost revised, so that the question on the December 3, 1956, ballot was to approve a $13.5-million city hall. This time, by a majority of 31,557 "for" to 26,679 "against," the construction of Toronto's new city hall was approved.

With this mandate Phillips then took another controversial step and ordered that, rather than relying on design submissions prepared only by

Not long after Nathan Phillips was elected Toronto's new mayor in 1955, he began promoting a new city hall to replace the "ancient" municipal building at the top of Bay Street. This sketch depicts an idea put forward by a consortium of distinguished Canadian architectural firms. With Toronto now part of the recently created Municipality of Metropolitan Toronto, it was thought best that the two levels of government share the proposed new building.

Canadian architects, a truly international competition would be held. As a result of the mayor's controversial decision, Toronto was fortunate to get Finnish architect Viljo Revell's masterpiece as its new city hall.

PIGOTT
where construction is a career

The Pigott Construction Company has become widely known for successful on-time completion of some of Canada's most impressive building projects. Access to critical materials even in periods of scarcity, extensive company-owned resources of construction equipment, and highly trained personnel . . . all have contributed to this record of achievement.

The Pigott Construction Company is the General Contractor for the new Head Office of Imperial Oil Limited on St. Clair Avenue West in Toronto . . . Mathers and Haldenby, Architects. With 19 storeys plus penthouse above and three storeys below street level, it will house 1000 employees in one of the most modern office buildings in North America.

Imperial Oil Building, Toronto
Superintendent of Construction on this building project is Alex. Farquhar. He joined Pigott Construction in 1928 and his experience has included every phase of the construction business.

PIGOTT CONSTRUCTION COMPANY LTD.

Look familiar? In this March 18, 1957, newspaper ad placed by the project's general contractor, the new Imperial Oil Building on St. Clair Avenue West looked surprisingly like the new city hall proposal put forward two years earlier.

But back to the consortium's concept for the building that had appeared in the November 1955 newspaper article. When a new head office for Imperial Oil was proposed to replace the company's cramped quarters in an old office building at the northwest corner of Church and King streets, officials called on the architectural firm of Mathers and Haldenby, one of the trio of firms that prepared plans for the proposed new Toronto city hall back in 1955. As can be seen in the March 18, 1957, newspaper ad that extolled the virtues of the new Imperial Oil Building on St. Clair, elements from that earlier project were "recycled."

Today, the building has been converted into a condominium appropriately named the Imperial Plaza.

October 31, 2010

Lavish Houses of Government

Newspaper headline: Opposition Speakers Continued to Press Their Criticisms Against the Policy of the Government in Making Lavish Expenditures.

Now, before you think that this statement refers to a recently published article, let me tell you that it actually appeared in a newspaper story dated June 19, 1914! The "lavish expenditures" referred to had to do with the $1.25 million that the Conservative government had placed in

Over a period of nearly a century and a half the province has had four Government Houses. This "ancient" postcard depicts the third version that stood at the southwest corner of King and Simcoe streets from 1868. It was demolished in 1912.

the estimates for a new Government House that would serve the needs of Ontario's lieutenant governor. And that figure was just for the structure. The property in Rosedale on which the structure would be built was sure to add another $150,000 to the estimate, with another $110,000 added for landscaping. And then there was a yet undetermined amount for fixtures and furnishings. However, as hard as the opposition fought against the new vice-regal residence, work continued and it opened for business in late 1915.

It wasn't long before this Government House, a fifty-seven-room mansion that was the fourth (and last) to be built in the province to serve the British monarch's representative in Ontario, took on the title Chorley Park. That soubriquet was only natural, since the land on which it was built had been the private garden of Toronto businessman and "founder" of the city's public library system John Hallam. He named his property that overlooked the Don Valley after his birthplace, Chorley, a town in Lancashire, England.

The fourth Government House stood in Rosedale and was first occupied in 1915. Usually referred to as Chorley Park, it ceased to be the home of the lieutenant governor in 1937, and after being used for a number of other purposes was unceremoniously torn down twenty-four years later. The area remains a park.

Chorley Park served as the vice-regal residence until Mitch Hepburn and his Ontario Liberal Party (the party that had fought the idea of building the place back when it was first proposed) gained power in July of 1934. Within three years the Liberals had seen to it that Chorley Park was no longer used as a government building. For the first time since Peter Hunter (the province's second lieutenant governor, who served from 1799–1805 and whose official residence and office was in a small wood-frame house on the grounds of today's Fort York) held the post, the province was without a Government House.

Over the next few years little maintenance was done and the mansion slowly deteriorated. But with the outbreak of the Second World War it was painfully obvious that the country was ill-equipped to look after the hundreds of returning wounded. The old military hospital on Christie Street was overcrowded with veterans of the Great War and a proposed new military hospital (to be known as the Toronto War Memorial Hospital and built well north of the city on the former Sunnybrook Farm property in the Township of North York) was still years in the future. So the former Government House in Rosedale was converted into a convalescent hospital, with the last patient moving out in 1952.

In 1955, members of the RCMP moved in, but by that time the place was in such bad shape that the Mounties only stayed one year. The next tenants were a group of university students who had fled their homeland during the Hungarian Revolution in 1958. The following year the city purchased the rapidly deteriorating building for $100,000. Some of the politicians had ideas that it would make a fitting cultural centre, but when presented with the estimated cost to refurbish and bring the forty-four-year-old building up to code, they quickly abandoned the plan. Other ideas were put forward, none of which were acceptable, except for one that is: Simply pay a local wrecking company six thousand dollars to have the old structure demolished. Then turn the property into a public park. All in favour say "Aye."

Carried.

November 14, 2010

The History of Sick Kids

When Toronto was still a very young city, what we know today as University Avenue was actually made up of two separate, dirt-covered thoroughfares, one quite narrow and the other considerably wider. They both began at Queen Street and ran north to College. The street on the east was a public thoroughfare called Park Lane, and it fronted Osgoode Hall and a selection of small houses that lined the east side of the narrow street all the way north to College Street.

Immediately to the west was the much wider College Avenue. It was a private roadway controlled by the officials of King's College, a school of higher learning that had been established in 1829. This street came complete with a gatehouse at the southernmost end (Queen Street) and a gatekeeper who controlled access to the road and to the land north to the King's College building that stood on the site of today's Ontario Legislative Building (Queen's Park).

In 1949, the school was renamed the University of Toronto, and the following year the beautiful new University College, located a little farther west, was opened for business. Old King's College was then put to other uses, not the least of which was as an insane asylum. But that was years before the provincial politicians moved into their new building, which had been erected on the site in the early 1890s.

Eventually, Park Lane and the College Avenue became one and

the present University Avenue name was adopted. However, it was the ravages of the Great Depression in the early 1930s that prompted Toronto politicians to have the avenue extended several blocks south of Queen, down to Front Street. To accomplish this, many desperate men were given a pick and shovel so that they could earn enough money to provide their families with food and lodging.

Before the new Sick Kids Hospital could be built, it was necessary to remove this trailer camp that was located on the east side of University Avenue at Gerrard.

The Victorian Hospital for Sick Children was erected at the southeast corner of College and Elizabeth streets in the early 1890s. Today, the handsome old landmark is home to the Canadian Blood Services.

This souvenir postcard shows the new Hospital for Sick Children soon after it opened at its new site on University Avenue in early 1951.

One of the most impressive buildings on today's University Avenue is the world-famous Hospital for Sick Children. The first Sick Kids occupied an old building just off University, not far from where Toronto General Hospital is today. It opened in 1875, and was followed a few years later by a slightly larger facility nearby. Then, thanks to the generosity of the founder of the *Evening Telegram* newspaper, John Ross Robertson, a modern (for the day) hospital building was erected on College Street just east of University at Elizabeth Street.

But as the city continued to grow, so too did the need for a new, larger children's hospital. With the war recently over, a site for the new hospital was selected at the southeast corner of University and Gerrard Street. However, there was a problem: A severe lack of wartime housing throughout the city in the early 1940s had resulted in Toronto's only trailer camp having been spontaneously established on the vacant lot. With no place to relocate the dozens of so-called "trailer dwellers," the city was reluctant to force them off the future hospital site. It wasn't until alternate sites could be found for them that work on the new hospital could proceed. The new Hospital for Sick Children at 555 University Avenue opened in early 1951.

November 28, 2010

Shedding Light on a Landmark

Recognized by those in the know as the oldest existing lighthouse on the Great Lakes, and believed by many to be one of the oldest in the country, Toronto's Gibraltar Point Lighthouse on Toronto Island

Today, the Gibraltar Point Lighthouse sits high and dry, far from the water's edge and, some say, all alone with its "ghost."

was erected in 1808, a mere fifteen years after the city of Toronto was established as the Town of York. The original structure was built of stone that was barged across Lake Ontario from a quarry in Queenston and stood sixteen metres (fifty-three feet) in height at the west end of the peninsula (the island didn't come into existence until a furious storm split the peninsula from the mainland in 1858) and stood a few yards north of the Lake Ontario shoreline.

In 1832, the structure grew to 19.6 metres (64.3 feet) with the addition of stone from a different quarry, this one in Kingston.

Allowing for the height of the lantern enclosure, the overall height of the lighthouse was now twenty-five metres (eighty-two feet), high enough to be seen from the lake by schooners bound for the Port of Toronto.

In the beginning, the light (originally white, then later green) was produced by burning sperm whale oil and later coal oil. The lamp assembly was converted to electricity following the 1916–17 season. The light was finally extinguished at the end of the 1957 shipping season, but the lighthouse still stands today, a relic from Toronto's past.

Visitors to the Gibraltar Point Lighthouse often ask two questions: Why would the point be called Gibraltar Point when it's nowhere near the Mediterranean? And why would anyone erect a lighthouse so far from the water?

Well, it was John Graves Simcoe, the province's first lieutenant governor, who gave the point of land near the future site of the lighthouse the name Gibraltar Point. In doing so he was describing that location (tongue planted firmly in cheek, no doubt) as being as easily defensible against invaders (referring to the hated Americans) as was Gibraltar at the entrance to the Mediterranean Sea.

This rare aerial photograph shows the Gibraltar Point Lighthouse nearly surrounded by water in the early 1900s. Note the city skyline in the background with the tower of the still-new city hall visible to the left of centre.

And the answer to the second question: Why would a lighthouse be constructed so far from the edge of the lake? That's easy. When the lighthouse was built, it *was* close to the edge of the lake. As the years passed, officials took steps to increase the land mass of the island. As a result of this landfill, the lighthouse seemed to recede inland.

And then there's the question of the ghost, the one that many insist is the ethereal remains of the first lighthouse keeper. For nearly two centuries it has been rumoured that it was on January 2, 1815, that J.P. Radan Muller (or is it Rademüller? The actual spelling is just one of the imprecise facts in this case) was murdered in the lighthouse. Ancient rumours suggest that the deed was committed by two members of the military stationed at the garrison across the bay after the keeper refused their demand for liquor from his plentiful supply. What *is* known for sure is that Radan Muller was never seen again. Years later it was reported that human remains were found near the base of the lighthouse, but their identity was never confirmed.

January 2, 2011

Fire-Claimed Landmarks

It wasn't long after fire broke out in the almost 125-year-old former Empress Hotel at the intersection of Yonge and Gould in downtown Toronto that it became obvious the city was about to lose yet another of its few remaining heritage structures. This time it would be a building that had already been recognized as having architectural merit, and had been designated as such in August 2010 by Toronto City Council. However, as a result of bureaucratic ineptness and/or indifference the site had been left unprotected. And whether it turns out to be demolition by neglect, or, as seems more likely, as a result of arson,* the fact is that another piece of our city's past is gone forever.

In 1927, the Provincial Improvement Corp. released this sketch of the amusement pier proposed for the mouth of the Humber River. It was to be built on the site of the present Palace Pier & Palace Place condominium complex.

It was on January 9, 1963, that we lost another of our long-time landmarks. And while it wasn't quite as old as the Empress (later Edison) Hotel, the Palace Pier, a popular dance hall and multi-purpose facility on the Lake Ontario shoreline at the mouth of the Humber River, had a remarkable history. That history lasted until the day when it, too, was ravaged by fire, a fire that was later discovered to have been deliberately set.

The Palace Pier was the brainchild of the Provincial Improvement Corporation, a group of well-healed businessmen who had the idea that a pier similar to those that ringed the British Isles and made their shareholders a lot of money could do the same thing here in Toronto. Actually the Toronto project wasn't exactly *in* Toronto, but rather across the Humber and legally in the Township of Etobicoke. But that didn't matter. The new pier's proximity to the amazingly popular Sunnyside Amusement Park, which had drawn thousands to its games and rides since its opening in 1922, would all but guarantee big bucks for any and all shareholders in what was to be known far and wide as the Palace Pier. It was to be almost 550 metres (1,800 feet) in length and be lined with restaurants, rides, a large bandstand, a one-thousand-seat theatre and a mammoth dance hall

Reader Alex Bauldry sent along a copy of this $10 share issued by the Dominion Palace Pier Corp. promoters in 1929. When too few shares were purchased the grand master plan underwent a major revision.

with space for three thousand couples to dance the night away. In addition, there would be several large meeting rooms to accommodate convention groups that would arrive at docking facilities provided for passenger ships from all around the Great Lakes. There was no doubt that the proposed Palace Pier would have it all and work got underway with the laying of the traditional cornerstone in early January 1931.

A descriptive plaque has been installed on all that's left of one of the Palace Pier's footings.

Unfortunately, what the promoters didn't see coming was a worldwide depression that soon ended any chance of raising two-million-dollars-worth of ten-dollar shares from the general public. As a result, the company's grand plan for a mammoth pier was scaled back and a structure only ninety metres (three hundred feet) in length was completed. But even that venture was unsuccessful, and another nine years would pass before the new Strathcona Palace Pier opened as a roller rink. It's first skater? Comedian Bob Hope, who was in town promoting his new movie *Caught in the Draft* at the Uptown Theatre and signing autographs at the British Bomb Victims' fundraising event sponsored by the Canadian Red Cross and held at the Manning Depot at the CNE grounds. The first public event was a Christmas Eve dance presented two years later at what was by that time called the Queensway Palace Pier.

For several years, many popular big bands frequented the venue, and when their popularity waned the owners started booking wrestling matches, high-school dances, and labour meetings at the hall.

Then, sometime early on the morning of January 9, 1963, some "citizen" set the place on fire. Before long the Toronto newspapers were receiving queries from employees at the Buffalo papers wondering what the red glow in the sky over Toronto was.

It was the reflection of a dying city landmark.

January 9, 2011

* In July 2012, an individual was arrested and subsequently charged with setting the fire that destroyed the former Empress Hotel on January 3, 2011.

Canadian Icon's Birthplace

Frequently I'll look at an old photograph and after a few minutes determine that I've seen everything that's been captured in the view. Such was the case with the old black and white photograph from the City of Toronto Archives that accompanies this column. Then, for whatever reason, I decided to take a second look. Especially at the sign at the far left side of the view. Look closely and you too can see the words *poration limited* and beside that *res & tubes cut rates*.

Now, you may ask what's so special about those few, mostly undecipherable words. The answer requires a little history about the property and the building to which the sign is attached. As recorded in the book *Freewheeling* by Ian Brown, the little garage at the southeast corner of Gerrard and Hamilton streets (and opposite the old Don Jail) was initially occupied by the Hamilton Tire and Rubber Company. In the early fall of 1922, the business was purchased by John Billes and his younger brother Alfred for $1,800. One of the reasons that the purchase price was so low may have been that the original owners realized that business would be badly affected when the street in front of their garage was closed to all traffic in July 1922 while the old Gerrard Street bridge over the Don River was being replaced with a new $762,000 one.

For this reason they got quite a deal, but unfortunately the bridge construction went on for eighteen months and the street didn't reopen

Looking west along Gerrard Street from just west of Broadview Avenue, 1922. The street was closed as construction progressed on a new bridge across the Don River. At the extreme left side of the old photo is the sign that I believe reads in its entirety CANADIAN TIRE CORPORATION LIMITED TIRES & TUBES CUT RATES.

A similar view today. A city parking lot now occupies the former automobile service station that grew into today's Canadian Tire, the nation's largest retailer with nearly five hundred stores across Canada.

until mid-December of the following year. For obvious reasons, their tire and repair business was badly affected. In fact, business was so bad that they decided to move, first to a shop at Yonge and Gould (across Gould Street from the late fire-ravaged Empress, later Edison Hotel) and shortly thereafter to a building at the northeast corner of Yonge and Isabella. In 1927, business was so good that another, larger building was chosen and a fourth move was made to the southeast corner of the same intersection.

Now, here's where that sign on the side of the Gerrard and Hamilton streets building comes into play. Virtually all the references to the history of today's mighty Canadian Tire empire suggest that the Canadian Tire name didn't become visible to the public until the boys had moved the business into this latter property.

However, I submit that the name was already there for all to see on that much earlier Gerrard Street garage and can be deciphered from the letters *poration limited* visible in the old photo. They form a portion of the title Canadian Tire Corporation Limited (with the words *Tubes & Tires* added). If I'm correct, this city parking lot is the birthplace of what has grown into Canada's largest retailer. An historic plaque on the site perhaps?

January 16, 2011

Postcards from the Edge of Town

As I'm sure most of my readers know, there are clubs and organizations that specialize in virtually everything and anything that's collectible. Take the ordinary picture postcard, for instance. Now pretty much relegated to the "wish you were here" tourism trade, there was a time when these cards were important forms of communication, and with the earliest cards costing but a single penny, it was an inexpensive way to keep in touch. However, for many collectors, including myself, it's what was on the other side that was all important.

The most interesting cards feature skyline views, office and bank buildings (which were usually brand new when the card was created), and street scenes (some with automobiles sketched in to make the town look more important). Almost all of these old picture postcards were beautifully hand-coloured, most often by an artist in Europe, which is one of the reasons why the colours don't usually match the real thing. One of the early 1900s cards in my collection depicts a Toronto streetcar sporting a green livery. Obviously the artist, who was working for the huge J. Valentine & Co. postcard manufacturing concern in Dundee, Scotland, had never visited our fair city.

Another interesting genre of postcard is exemplified by the one that accompanies this column. It was loaned to me by Kyle Joliffe, an active member of the Toronto Postcard Club (*torontopostcardclub.com*).

As you ramble on thru Life, Brother, Whatever be your Goal, & keep your Eye upon the Doughnut And not upon the Hole!

This picture was sent to me by Kyle Joliffe, a member of the Toronto Postcard Club. It's typical of the fascinating images from the past that card collectors find in the strangest places. The statement on the card was posted in all Downyflake shops.

One of the most popular Downyflake donut and coffee shops was this one located on the north side of Lake Shore Boulevard and adjacent to the even more popular Sunnyside Amusement Park. The busy Roncesvalles, King, Queen, and Lakeshore Road intersection is (though it's now missing the latter roadway) located high on the hill in the background.

It features an image I remember first seeing when I was a kid growing up just south of the Bloor and Bathurst intersection.

Located on the north side of Bloor, squeezed between the corner and the Alhambra Theatre was a Downyflake donut shop. What caught the eye of passersby was the little machine in the window that cranked out hundreds of little round donuts as they watched — à la Tiny Tom's at the CNE.

January 23, 2011

Hustled by City Hall

Toronto-born architect Edward James Lennox (1854–1933) already had a number of his hometown's buildings to his credit when he was approached by city officials in 1886 to enter a competition to design a new municipal building for the fast-growing metropolis. This was actually the second of two competitions for this project, which had called for a set of architectural plans for a new courthouse as well. The first time around no one was interested. Officials then approached Lennox. The thirty-two-year-old accepted the challenge, and while it seemed like a simple enough project at the time, little did Lennox know that by taking on this assignment he was setting himself up for months of frustration followed by years of litigation.

Edward James Lennox, architect of Toronto's beautiful "old" city hall. It took years for E.J. to get paid.

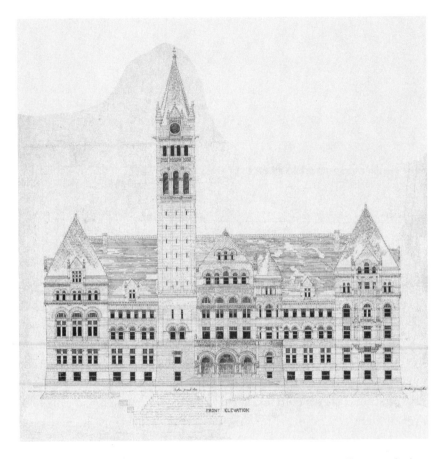

This 1887 sketch depicts the "new" city hall that was to be built in Toronto. A close look will show that it was different in several ways from what was actually completed a dozen years later. The most obvious is the height of the tower.

The problems all started when Lennox's plans for the courthouse were ordered changed in mid-stream. He was told to alter them and to design a combination courthouse and city hall instead. Over the next few years many additional changes were requested, each change resulting in more money from the taxpayers. However, after dozens of meetings, no actual work on the new building had taken place. In fact, another three years would pass before Lennox's plans were considered acceptable to allow work on the new and much altered building to finally start. By then, 1889, the cost had doubled from the original $300,000 to $600,000.

In 1896, another $200,000 was added to this latter figure in order, as was recorded, "to complete the new Court House and City Hall." Now the figure was $800,000. The next year another $275,000 was added to the total, this time "to further complete the City and County Buildings and

Souvenir postcard of architect Lennox's city hall when it was still the "new" city hall.

to furnish same." Interestingly, it was at this point in the project's lengthy evolution that architect Lennox, fed up with the building contractor's lack of zeal in getting the job done, fired him and took over supervising the massive job himself.

As the building slowly took shape, the city's accountants once again examined the books and determined that adding in the cost of the land on which the building was being erected had boosted the project cost to exactly $2,124,992.27. When Lennox's masterpiece was officially opened two years later the bill had risen by another $400,000.

Many taxpayers breathed a sigh of relief, believing that what had started out as a $300,000 building and had escalated to $2.5 million was finally complete.

But wait a minute. There was another bill. This one was submitted by the architect and one-time building contractor, Edward James Lennox. While he had already received $61,000 from the city, Lennox wanted more, lots more. In fact, he wanted $208,000 more. And he had the documents to support his request. Having spent far more time on the project than he expected, working as both architect and project contractor, Lennox felt his request for payment of that amount was fully justified.

Of course, the city disagreed, and before long the architect and city officials found themselves in court. For more than a decade arguments were made over what Lennox should be paid. Finally, in January of 1912, his request for $208,000 was met with a counter offer of just $20,000. That figure was quickly rejected and the city, rather sheepishly, raised that figure to $60,000. Still not what the architect wanted.

But by now Lennox was tired of fighting the municipal bureaucracy. Plus he had a new project that needed all his attention, a place that would be known as Casa Loma. Lennox reluctantly accepted the city's latest offer, making the total payment he would receive for one of the city's most impressive landmarks, and a project that took twenty-six years out of his career, a mere $121,000.

February 6, 2011

This Victoria Square Just a Dream

This artist's concept of the proposed Victoria Square project appeared in Toronto newspapers on April 9, 1900. The street at the bottom left is Richmond, and running across the bottom from the lower right is James Street, shown extended south from Queen to connect with Richmond. Queen Street, with its ubiquitous streetcars, crosses in front of the brand new city hall. The tall structure to the left is the IOF Building, while in the centre of the proposed Victoria Square is a huge statue honouring the reigning Queen Victoria.

In the previous column I described how Edward James Lennox, architect of Toronto's "old" city hall (1899–1966), spent years trying to get the city to hand over the money he felt he was owed for the extra time and effort he put in to not only designing, but overseeing the construction of one of the city's finest landmarks. In the long run he was unsuccessful, receiving less than half of the $280,000 he had demanded.

Even as Lennox's city hall was taking shape, a group of prominent businessmen began discussing a plan to create a huge public space in front of the new structure. This open space, to be known as Victoria Square, would be bounded by Queen, Bay, and Richmond streets on the north, west, and south side respectively. Closing the square on the east would be James Street, which would be extended south from Queen to connect with Richmond. All the existing buildings within the new square would be demolished.

A "crowning" feature would be a mammoth statue of the reigning and much-loved Queen Victoria, to be erected right in the centre of this impressive new addition to the city's downtown.

Had Victoria Square materialized, most of the ancient buildings in and around the Queen and Bay corner, seen here photographed from the lawn of the then new city hall, would have been demolished. The tall structure is the IOF Building (also known as the Temple Building) at the northwest corner of Bay and Richmond. Erected in 1895, it was one of the city's first "skyscrapers," but was demolished in 1970.

As we now know, the project went nowhere. Because, while there was lots of talk, it wasn't long before the matter of the necessary dollars and cents came into play. Not helping was the projected loss of assessment income from all the existing buildings that would have to be demolished.

In 1902, a somewhat less impressive statue honouring Queen Victoria was unveiled in front of the Ontario Legislature Building. Victoria had passed away the year before.

Before long the project became just a fanciful memory.

However, when Queen Victoria died in 1901, the idea of a memorial was rekindled, and while she never made it onto a throne in the heart of the "Queen City," the following year she was given a place of honour just to the east of the main entrance to the Ontario Legislative Building at Queen's Park.

February 13, 2011

Arrow's Short-Lived Flights

"Black Friday" refers to the day in 1959 that the federal government, under Prime Minister John Diefenbaker, put an end to one of Canada's greatest achievements in the field of aviation, the untouchable (for the day) Avro Arrow. The aircraft's fans and critics continue to debate whether the sudden and unexpected demise of the Arrow was in the nation's best interest, and it's quite likely that this difference of opinion will always remain.

When word got out that the Royal Canadian Air Force was looking for new jet interceptor, people began speculating on what it would look like. This concept appeared in the September 26, 1957, edition of the *Toronto Telegram* newspaper.

The Avro Arrow was seen as the replacement aircraft for the RCAF's CF-100 jet fighter. The plane had been developed in the late 1940s by the talented staff at the Avro Canada plant located adjacent to what was then known as Malton Airport and today as Toronto Pearson International Airport.

Eight days after the newspaper sketch of the RCAF's proposed new fighter appeared, the real thing was rolled out. I obtained this great photo from long-time friend David Reppen, one of the numerous Avro employees present at the historic October 4, 1957, event.

The Avro Arrow's premier test pilot was the legendary Jan Zurakowski. His story is told in Bill Zuk's book *Janusz Zurakowski: Legends in the Sky* (Vanwell Publishing, 2004).

The twin-engine CF-100 first flew in early 1950 and for more than a decade it criss-crossed the skies above Canada, protecting us and our American allies against attack by hoards of manned bombers of the mighty Russian air force. Though such attacks never materialized, one only has to have lived through those times to understand just how important this aerial protection was in keeping our free world free.

As the possibility of nuclear war heated up, it soon became obvious that a much improved interceptor would be necessary. Thanks to the technical expertise available within Avro Canada's workforce, a revolutionary new interceptor was born. With flying characteristics that exceeded anything produced thus far by any of the other allied nations, the new CF-105 Avro Arrow was described by many in the know as the world's best.

But it was costly — too costly, many believed, for a small nation like Canada. Attempts were made to have other countries add the Arrow to their military arsenals. That would have brought the cost per aircraft down. But no allied air force was interested. And then there was the question of missiles roaring through space to intercept the intruders. Would these unmanned missiles do the job better than the Arrow? And do it faster? And cheaper? Were manned aircraft obsolete? And would space be the next battlefield?

As if to emphasize this last point, the world's first space satellite, something called "Sputnik," which was developed by our sworn enemies, the Russians, went into low Earth orbit on October 4, 1957 — the same day that the first Avro Arrow emerged from its top secret hangar. Arrow RL201 would make its maiden flight on March 25, 1958, with the legendary test pilot Jan Zurakowski at the controls. The first Arrow was followed by four more, all of which pushed the revolutionary aircraft's flying characteristics higher and higher.

Then came Friday, February 20, 1959. With virtually no warning, the PA system in the Avro factory blared, ordering all staff to put their tools down and clear all buildings ... immediately. Work on the Arrow project came to a standstill. Quickly, all five Arrows, as well as those in various stages of completion, along with all special tools, diagrams, and manuals, were destroyed. The Avro Arrow dream was over.

February 20, 2011

He Was the Justin Bieber of '52

One day, while skimming through the numerous stations on our new flat-screen TV, I came across news coverage of a recent Justin Bieber concert. I'm always amazed at the reaction of the youngsters in the crowd at this kind of event, and while I don't pretend to understand it, I do remember the time I worked at the CNE and was caught up (literally) in a throng of teenagers who rushed the Grandstand stage at an Osmonds concert in the summer of 1974. There were a few scary moments, until several burly police officers got several of us off to one side and out of the way.

A few of this column's more mature readers may recall an occasion back in February 1952 when a performer (who could perhaps be described as the "Justin Bieber of the 1950s") appeared on a stage here in Toronto. Nicknamed "Mr. Emotion," twenty-five-year-old singer Johnnie Ray broke all box office records when he appeared at a local combination vaudeville and movie house called the Casino.

The theatre had opened in 1936 as a burlesque house and was located on the south side of Queen Street, almost in the middle of the Bay to York block. In later years, and under the management of Murray Little, the Casino became *the* place in Toronto to see and be entertained by an incredible array of movie stars (some on their way up the ladder, most on their way down), a few sports figures like Jack Dempsey, and a huge array of musical talents, including Bill Haley and the Comets, the Ink Spots,

Victor Borge (his first Canadian appearance was at the Casino), Louis Armstrong, Hank Snow, and, of course, Johnnie Ray. The latter appeared in Toronto during the week of February 21–27, 1952, while Ray was still riding high on the Hit Parade with his two chart-topping recordings,

Singing superstar Johnnie Ray greets his fans at the back door of the Casino Theatre, February 22, 1952.

"Cry" and "The Little White Cloud that Cried." Incidentally, Toronto's fabulous Four Lads, St. Michael's Choir School grads, can be heard on both songs. The boys were soon to be chart-toppers themselves.

To underline Johnnie Ray's popularity, Murray Little's son Barry told me that even before the Casino box office opened to start selling tickets for Ray's week-long appearance, people were lining up along the south side of Queen Street on both sides of the theatre from Bay on the east to York on the west. Up until then no performer had ever drawn that kind of crowd.

Now, here's the connection with Canada's Justin Bieber, tentative as it may be. In a column that appeared on February 28, 1952, legendary Toronto newspaper columnist Frank Tumpane described his visit to the Casino Theatre to see for himself those "Rayving Maniacs" (get it … *Ray*-ving?) seated in the audience to take in Johnnie Ray's performance. Frank described what he saw:

The south side of Queen Street between Bay and York streets as it appeared in the early 1960s. Note the two theatres, the Broadway (left), and farther west the Festival Cinema, the new name for the Casino. The Sheraton Centre now occupies this stretch of Queen Street.

He is the current outstanding example of that modern phenomenon, the vocalist who is able to induce a form of mass hysteria among young girls. I watched him do this and it is an awesome sight. At the performance the first half dozen rows were filled with junior misses. Many of them carried high school books under their arms and had obviously skipped school to hear their idol. The effect of his singing on the young girls was awesome. The squeals rise again and again almost drowning out the words of the singer. When the performance ended the house lights were turned on and attempts made to clear the theatre so the waiting crowds could get in.

And remember, he was describing a Johnnie Ray concert, not one featuring Justin Bieber.

February 27, 2011

Arcade Building a T.O. Original

On March 6, 1834, what had been established in 1793 as the Town of York was officially given city status. Along with the requisite royal assent came a name change, from York (selected by John Graves Simcoe to honour Frederick, the Duke of York, the second-eldest son of King George III) to a name that had identified the area long before the town was established. And while we don't know the exact derivation of the word (and there are more than a dozen possibilities to choose from) the world knows that wonderful city today as Toronto.

It was in the spring of 1883, and as a kind of present to Toronto as it approached its fiftieth anniversary, David Blain, the president of the Ontario Loan and Investment Company, announced that his organization was prepared to spend almost $100,000 on the construction of a building that he said would be the only one of its kind anywhere in the country.

Designed by local architect Charles Walton, the company's new "Arcade Building" would be erected on the east side of Yonge Street, almost mid-block between Richmond and Adelaide streets. The east and west ends would be four storeys high while the centre section would be three. The upper two floors would be ringed with forty-eight business offices. But what would really make the building special would be a main floor arcade or pedestrian walkway that would run between Yonge and Victoria streets, directly in line with Temperance Street to the west and Lombard Street to the east.

Looking north on Yonge Street from Adelaide, circa 1890. Just to the right of centre is the unique (for the time) Arcade Building, which opened in 1884. Today this site is occupied by a modern building that retains the historic Arcade name.

Courtesy of Vince McAuliffe.

Interior view of the Arcade Building showing some of the various small shops located on the three levels.

Lining both sides of this arcade would be a total of twenty-four shops, twelve on each side. This arrangement had never been attempted in any other Canadian retail situation, although the layout was well-known across Europe and in various American cities.

The men behind the unusual project felt that by bringing together a wide assortment of businesses in one location they could collectively go up against the established stores of stalwart businessmen Timothy Eaton and Robert Simpson, who had held a monopoly on the "department store" business since 1869 and 1872 respectively. The idea worked extremely well and the Yonge Street Arcade opened in late 1884, remaining a landmark Toronto shopping destination for almost seven decades.

I have personal memories of the old building when, as a youngster, my mother would take her two boys to the Arcade's magic shop, where Bob and I would be dazzled and bewildered by the iconic Johnny Giordmaine. For many Christmases, Johnny was a fixture in Eaton's Toyland, and it was during this time that my mother got to know him personally, having met Johnny during her years working at Eaton's before she married my dad.

In this view, looking east along Temperance Street toward Yonge, the Arcade Building is shown after it underwent major alterations following a fire in 1953.

Sadly, a serious fire that erupted early on the morning of February 27, 1953, financially drained nearly fifty of the building's merchants and would ultimately lead to the closing and eventual demolition of the aged structure.

Interestingly, it wasn't until Phase One of the new Eaton Centre opened in early 1977 that anything came close to replicating the unique shopping theory pioneered by the Toronto Arcade.

A modern Arcade Building opened on the site in 1960 and still stands today.

March 6, 2011

Making Tracks Back to Belt Line

Each time I read or hear about the continuing expansion of our present GO transit system, I think about what must have been going through the minds of the developers of what was known as the Belt Line Railway. This interesting enterprise was established in the early 1890s by several pioneering Toronto businessmen who formed the Belt Land Corporation. The railway was intended to provide a commuter steam train service to and from a variety of suburban housing sites that the entrepreneurs would build throughout the suburban hinterland north of Toronto.

As can be seen on the accompanying map, the trains would enter and depart the old Union Station following tracks east and west across the waterfront, north and south through the Don Valley, east and west adjacent to a concession road we know as Eglinton Avenue, then to and from the waterfront via a routing well west of Dufferin Street. A second, shorter loop was built through the valley of the Humber River.

The first trains began operating in 1892 and within twenty-eight months, thanks mainly to the collapse of the real estate market and an overly expensive fare system that demanded an extra twenty-five cents every time the train stopped at one of the Belt Line stations, the project was terminated for lack of passengers.

Having just emerged from the Don Valley, a Belt Line train passes under a bridge located in the Moore Park Ravine. (Sketches from the Belt Land Corporation's promotional booklet.)

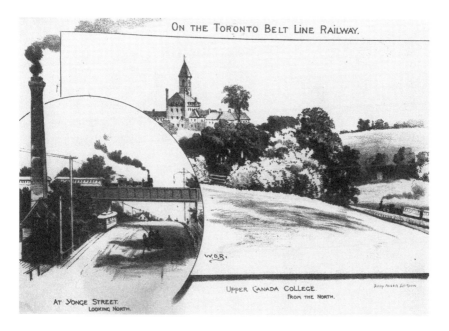

Where the Belt Line tracks crossed Yonge Street south of Merton. A portion of this bridge still stands. The TTC's Davisville subway yard is now located in behind the old power station chimney.

While the Belt Line trains may have vanished, a few miles of track continued to see use by the occasional freight train that served the Brick Works factory in the Don Valley. At the outbreak of the First World War, much of the remaining track was ripped up and used in the manufacture of explosives and shells.

Today, many kilometres of the Belt Line right-of-way have been incorporated into a series of unique walking trails that wind through the city.

April 10, 2011

The Vanishing Bayview Ghost

C lad in white brick, the structure that was to be officially known as the Hampton Court Apartments was a housing development that got caught up in a severe case of red tape*itis*. Its location on an elevated piece of property southwest of the Bayview Avenue and Nesbitt Drive intersection was a matter of prolonged discussions between municipal

Construction of the so-called "Bayview Ghost" began in 1959 on a rise of land just west of the north end of the Bayview Extension. It was to be a modern apartment building, but was to become a major real estate fiasco.

officials and the developer even before the first shovels were put in the ground in 1959. Impatient with the Leaside then the East York officials, the developer decided to go ahead with the project without waiting for all the necessary approvals.

No doubt upset with the developer's actions, municipal officials refused to provide either water or sewer connections for the building. A change in zoning rules also didn't help. Unfortunately for the builder, he had already started construction of the six-story building. When "stop work" orders were finally issued, only a shell of the building, as seen in the photo, had been constructed. Its white brick cladding soon gave rise to the ominous title, the "Bayview Ghost."

The "Ghost" remained a neighbourhood landmark for the next twenty-two years as it sat high and forlorn for all to see and wonder just what went wrong with an idea that seemed so right at the time. Demolition finally came in 1981, with East York mayor Alan Redway swinging the first blows. The Governor's Bridge Estates project (the governor referred to was the province's lieutenant governor who lived in a nearby, now-demolished mansion located in Chorley Park) was built on the site.

May 1, 2011

From Farm Field to Airfield

The twentieth century was just a few years old when young Toronto law clerk Fred Robins started his real estate company. Over the following years he built many subdivisions on the northern fringes of the city, one of which we know today as the popular Armour Heights neighbourhood. This subdivision actually began as Robin's suburban farm estate and one that he named "Strathrobyn." The play on his surname is interesting, as is the fact that his lovely residence remains today as the Canadian Forces College on Wilson Avenue.

Though Robins was too old to take part in the Great War in 1917, he eagerly offered a large area of his nearly four-hundred-acre farm for use as an airfield. The offer was favourably accepted by the Royal Flying Corps (Canada's air force didn't come into existence for another seven years) and in short order biplanes filled the skies over the new so-called Armour Heights Airfield. One of the visitors to the field was a young Amelia Earhart, who was a Canadian Red Cross nursing aid downtown and was drawn to the airfield by her love of flying machines.

Following the end of the war, the field was converted to a commercial flying field operated by Billy Bishop and Billy Barker, two of Canada's top aviation heroes. (The former recently had his name added to the airport on Toronto Island, while the latter was recognized many years ago in the name of a short-lived airport on the west side of Dufferin Street just north of Lawrence Avenue.)

Close inspection of the accompanying map reveals several present-day subdivisions, a few well-known city streets, a former as well as a present-day golf course, a portion of the route of the high-speed radial streetcar line from Toronto's northern city limits to Lake Simcoe, as well as the TTC's Yonge city streetcar loop at the south end of Hogg's Hollow.

Of special interest is the curving Yonge Boulevard, which was constructed to take traffic around the very steep Hogg's Hollow hill on Yonge Street. The construction of Highway 401 in the 1950s resulted in the boulevard ending just north of Wilson Avenue, and the bridge that took the original Yonge Boulevard over the Don Valley to connect with Yonge north of Hogg's Hollow was incorporated into the 401, where it remains in use to this day.

May 8, 2011

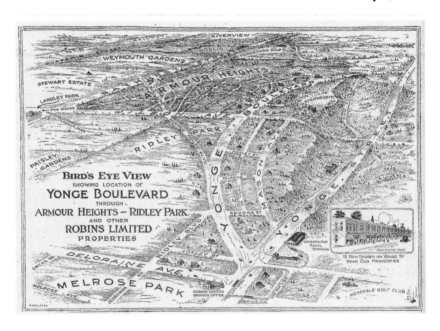

This map, dated April 1923, was prepared by prominent Toronto real estate company Robins Limited. What was developed into today's popular Armour Heights neighbourhood was originally a suburban farm estate owned by the company founder, Frederick Burton Robins. During the latter part of the First World War he turned the site over to the military for use as an airfield.

In this undated photo, one of the pilots in training "buzzes" the barracks at the Armour Heights airfield.

The Cyclorama Experience

In an earlier column I wrote about the "Bayview Ghost," a building that never achieved its destiny as an apartment building. Another Toronto building that ended its existence as something completely

Another interesting building from Toronto's past was the unusual Cyclorama. Erected in 1887 on the south side of Front Street just west of York, it began as an art gallery but ended up as a parking garage before being demolished in 1976. Photo circa 1922.

different from its intended use was the unique Cyclorama, a large, circular brick building that was erected in 1887 on the south side of Front Street, just west of the York Street corner (and opposite the foot of today's University Avenue).

This structure was Toronto's version of the extremely popular cycloramas of the day that could be found in cities around the world. In effect, these unique structures were really a combination art gallery/ amusement centre in which huge painted dioramas featuring a wide variety of historic events (the Battle of the Sedan, the Crucifixion, the Battle of Gettysburg, the Battle of Waterloo, etc.) lined the walls. After paying an admission fee, wide-eyed visitors would gaze upon the artwork as they made their way along specially built walkways threaded through the spectacular display. It was just like being there.

Before long, the Cyclorama experience was overtaken by the magic lantern, an early form of slide projector. Eventually this invention also became outdated following the introduction of silent films in hastily built moving picture theatres.

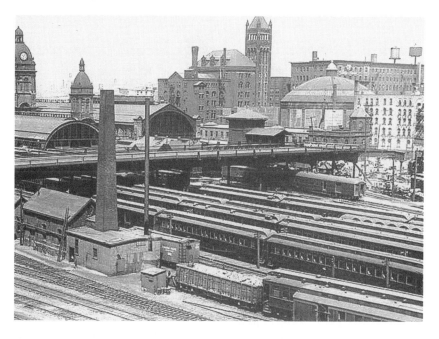

The Cyclorama, with its unique dome-like roof, is visible in the upper right corner of this 1926 view from the waterfront. Also visible is the old Union Station, which was in use prior to our present station opening in 1927.

In 1927, rather than demolishing the now-empty Cyclorama, the Petrie Machinery people bought it from the city and transformed it into a showroom as seen in the accompanying photo. Some years later, and in anticipation of parking requirements for the new Royal York Hotel then under construction nearby, the building was converted once again, this time into a unique 350-car parking garage that must have been a challenge even for the most talented drivers. Petrie then moved their operations into an old building near the northeast corner of Front and Bathurst streets, which in turn had an interesting history as the building in which the components of the Great Lakes passenger ship *Cayuga* were fabricated.

Finally, in September of 1976, both the Cyclorama and its neighbour immediately to the east, David Walker's historic Walker House Hotel, were demolished without a whimper. Citigroup Place now occupies the site.

May 22, 2011

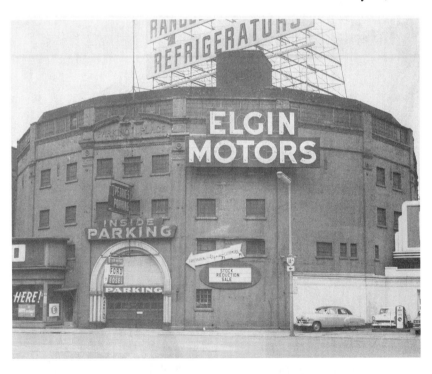

In anticipation of parking requirements for the new Royal York Hotel under construction nearby, the unusual building was converted into a 350-car parking garage.

That's One Big Birthday Candle

Months before any construction work began, the designers proposed a three-legged structure (as incorporated in this early model) that had the elevator incorporated inside the central tube. However, it was felt that the ride to the top could be marketed as one of the Tower's most interesting features and, as a result, the design was drastically changed. This allowed elevator passengers to experience incredible views of the city, the island, and, on clear days, the spray of Niagara Falls.

Next time you're at a party, strolling through a shopping centre, or riding the subway, take a look around you. Anyone you see who was born after 1976 has never known Toronto without the CN Tower gracing the city skyline. While it took almost forty months to build the structure, it was on June 26, 1976, that the CN Tower was opened to the general public.

Interestingly, the city's newest landmark actually had two openings, with the official event, complete with Prime Minister Pierre Trudeau in attendance, taking place more than three months later, on October 1. Numerous changes have taken place in and around the tower over the years. One that may surprise people is that it is no longer called the CN Tower, with CN recognizing the original owner, Canadian National Railway. Following the change of ownership in 1996, the initials CN now stand for "Canada's National" as in Canada's National Tower. Just thought you'd like to know.

Construction of the CN Tower began on February 6, 1973, and it didn't take long for the city's newest landmark to start taking shape. I took this photo in the summer of that same year and inadvertently captured not only the genesis of the new tower, but the price of parking in the lot on the northeast corner of Front and John streets: $1.25 per stay between 7:00 a.m. and 7:00 p.m.; 50 cents evenings or overnight after 5:00 p.m.; $18 per month, with in and out privileges. Note the massive wooden slipform into which huge amounts of concrete would be poured to help create the distinctive shape of the tower.

In the January 23, 1974, picture (below), the city's newest landmark soars skyward over a building that, while appearing unremarkable in this photo, would soon become another Toronto attraction. The mammoth new Toronto Terminal Warehouse was erected adjacent to the water's edge at the foot of York Street in 1926–27. It served for many years as a cold-storage facility for goods arriving by freighter and awaiting shipment to a myriad of city retailers. In the early 1980s, plans were put forward to demolish the building. However, the fact that the structure was constructed of reinforced concrete (one of the first of its kind in the country to be) made it extremely difficult and costly to demolish. Fortunately, the new owners decided it would make more financial sense to completely renovate the building. The "new" Queen's Quay Terminal shopping mall/office condominium complex opened in 1983.

June 26, 2011

View from the ferry *Thomas Rennie*, January 23, 1974, less than a year after construction work on the CN Tower began.

Whatever Happened to Gas Wars?

It used to be that the first thing you tried to find out after getting up each morning was that particular day's weather. Now it's finding out the price of a litre of gasoline, because sure as shooting it's different from the price it was when you went to bed the night before.

Of course, there have been numerous suggestions put forward as to why the price keeps climbing. Some experts suggest a shortage of petroleum products or unrest in the world. Then there's the nice driving weather that results in the increased number of cars on the road.

And there's something else. I often wonder if the lack of competition amongst the present gasoline suppliers has anything to do with rising prices. Many will remember when stretches of Toronto's main streets were lined with a variety of gasoline companies. As a young driver I remember some of the big companies with names like Texaco, B-A, Fina, and White Rose as well as some of the off-brands such as Lion, Regent, Spur, Beaver, Joy, and the latter's successor, Premium. Frequently, in an effort to increase the sale of their respective products, the operators of many of these stations would drop the price of a gallon of gas. This usually resulted in a gasoline price war. Initially, the price drop would amount to a savings of only a few cents, but as the war heated up (as it usually did before the big suppliers finally stepped in) it was soon well worth your while searching out the bargains around town. This was especially true for me, a young driver still attending school and without a lot of extra spending money. For me these price wars were a godsend.

Supertest's ad published in a July 1959 edition of the *Toronto Telegram* newspaper made sure people were aware that if the attendant failed to wash the car's windshield and check the oil level the purchase was free.

Some readers may have noticed that I failed to mention Supertest in my list of gas companies on the streets of Toronto in the 1950s and '60s. That's because I wanted to describe an especially fond memory I have of the all-Canadian company that was established in London, Ontario, in 1923 and bought by BP Canada in 1971. The latter company was then purchased by Petro-Canada twelve years later.

Supertest had a small station on Mt. Pleasant Road near the top of the street on which I grew up. It was where I obtained one of my first jobs. I was hired to pump gas (if I could find the filler pipe), check the oil, and wash the car windshields, all three "must do" items as decreed by the Supertest Company. The co-owner of the station was Harry Norman, who sold me my first "real" car, a 1958 Hillman Minx. Harry's partner, Jan Wietzes, along with sons Bert and Eppie, opened Wietzes Motors, a successful Toyota dealership, now located on Dufferin Street just north of Steeles Avenue.

July 17, 2011

This small North Toronto Supertest station was operated by Harry Norman and Jan Wietzes and sat for years at the northeast corner of Mt. Pleasant Road and Broadway Avenue. It was here that a young Mike Filey learned to pump gas, wash windshields, and check the pressure in your tires. Note the Hillman sign. I had a 1958 Minx. And if I'm right that's a 1959 Plymouth at the garage door and a 1953 Oldsmobile on the left.

Sailing Back in Time

One of the photos that accompanies this column (below) came to me from a *Sunday Sun* reader. It shows a sailing ship in the old Yonge Street slip. I know the location is at the foot of Yonge Street because in the background you can see the old curved roof of the Great Western Railway station. It was located where the Sony (O'Keefe/ Hummingbird) Centre is today. On the back of the photo someone has identified the vessel in the view as a "replica of one of Christopher Columbus's trio of caravels *Nina*, *Pinta*, and *Santa Maria*" (the latter being Columbus's flagship) and had added the date 1893.

Moored in the old Yonge Street slip is a replica of the famous *Santa Maria*, one of the three caravels in which Christopher Columbus and his crew crossed the Atlantic Ocean on his voyage to the "New World" in 1492.

As a result of nearly a century of land filling all along the city's central waterfront today's Yonge Street slip is much further south than the original.

Replicas of the *Nina*, *Pinta*, and *Santa Maria* lying in the North River, New York City, on their way to the 1893 World's Fair in Chicago.

I was able to determine from the old newspapers that these vessels did, in fact, stop in Toronto while on their way from Spain via Lakes Ontario, Erie, and Michigan en route to the 1893 Columbian World's Fair in Chicago. The trio was invited to the event in recognition of the four hundredth anniversary of Columbus's crossing of the Atlantic.

However, there were a couple of things that didn't jive with the 1893 date on the photo. To help me get some answers, I contacted Jay Bascom, an expert on the history of Toronto's waterfront. He was sure the launch seen to the extreme right of the view was the Royal Canadian Yacht Club's *Kwasind*, which wasn't built until 1912. And the sign with the word *Canada* on it was most likely the Canada Steamship Line dock at the foot of Yonge. That iconic company wasn't established until 1913.

It soon became obvious that the date 1893 was wrong. So what year was the photo taken? Another search of the newspapers revealed that the three replica caravels returned to Toronto in the fall of 1913 on their return voyage from Chicago, where they had spent the previous decade. This time the route saw the ships travel back through the three Great Lakes, up the St. Lawrence River, south down the Atlantic coast, through the Panama Canal to the Pacific Ocean, then up the West Coast to San Francisco, the site of the Pan-Pacific Exposition to be held in 1915.

Further research revealed that in 1917 the replica *Santa Maria* was sold for $800 at an auction in Charlottetown, Prince Edward Island. Its subsequent disposition as well as that of the other two replicas is unknown.

July 24, 2011

Rocket Blast to the Past

On July 21, 2011, Toronto transit riders were introduced to the latest generation of subway trains to operate in our city. Known as the "Toronto Rocket" (TR) and built by Bombardier in its Thunder Bay, Ontario, factory, each of these new trains is made up of six articulated cars.

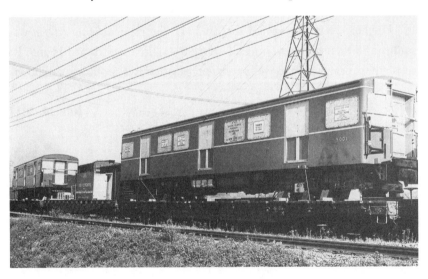

Built by the Gloucester Railway and Carriage Works in England, two of Toronto's original "red" subway cars are seen in transit from the Port of Montreal to Toronto on specially modified railway flat cars. The first two of the 106-car order — consisting of one hundred steel and six aluminum vehicles — arrived in the city on July 30, 1953.

Over the next few years seventy of these train sets (for a total of 420 cars) will replace the existing fleet of subway cars that have travelled millions of miles on the city's Yonge–University–Spadina and Bloor–Danforth lines.

The first of the new "TRs" (an interesting term that was also used to identify the old wooden streetcars of the Toronto Railway Company, the public transit operator that preceded the TTC) arrived at the Wilson Yard on October 1, 2010. The first train set was subject to months of testing before being entered into service in 2011.

Another interesting piece of Toronto subway trivia concerns the arrival of the TTC's very first subway cars. Many will remember those "red" cars. Manufactured by the Gloucester Railway Carriage and Wagon Co. in England, the first of the initial order for 106 of the cars (one hundred steel "red" cars and six weight-saving aluminum cars) arrived in Toronto on July 30, 1953. These "imported" vehicles were followed by an ever-increasing number of "homegrown" trains that were built by Montreal Locomotive Works and Hawker Siddeley, two Canadian companies that over time were acquired by Bombardier, the builder of the brand new "Toronto Rocket."

Courtesy of Mike DeToma, Toronto Transit Commission.

The first of Toronto's new generation of subway trains went into revenue service on July 21, 2011.

With the arrival of the Canadian-built equipment, the "red" cars were soon retired and scrapped, all except for cars 5098-5099 that is. They have been preserved and are on display at the Halton County Radial Railway Museum and Discovery Centre located northwest of Toronto. It's also worth noting that cars 5300-5301, the first Canadian-built subway cars, are also part of the museum's vast collection. This attraction has nearly seventy-five historic rail and transit artifacts on display (several of which are fully operational) and is well worth a family visit. All details can be found at *www.hcry.org.*

July 31, 2011

Debt, Generally Speaking

With the ongoing discussions about how to trim Toronto's massive debt, there have been numerous suggestions about which services to pare back on or eliminate altogether.

This circa 1910 postcard shows the Toronto General Hospital when it was on the north side of Gerrard Street, west of the Don River. This was the hospital's second location, the first being on King Street just west of John, and where the TIFF Bell Lightbox and Festival Tower complex stands today.

One of the institutions under the microscope has been the city's public library system, a treasured resource that has served Torontonians since its creation in 1883.

Historically, Toronto's free libraries were an extension of the first Mechanics' Institute that had been established in the Town of York three years before the community was given city status in 1834. The institute was described in literature of the day as being "libraries for the adult working class that provide an alternative pastime to gambling and drinking in pubs."

As unflattering as this statement may be, the real goal of the Mechanics' Institutes was to provide "adult education for the working classes, at no cost."

Financing of what were regarded as community amenities was undertaken by civic-minded businessmen who recognized the value of educating the citizens regardless of their ability to pay for the use of books as was demanded by the private libraries. The very first Mechanics' Institute was opened in Edinburgh, Scotland, in 1821, a mere ten years before ours.

In the early twentieth century, the city had several hospitals that served patients with specific illnesses. The one pictured here was once located high on the east side of the Don, north of the old Don Jail and west of Broadview Avenue. It was known locally as the Swiss Cottage and was the location of a smallpox hospital, where patients suffering from this highly contagious disease could be isolated from the public. It opened in 1901 and was intentionally burned to the ground in 1929.

Over the years, various attempts have been made to save money by eliminating books and branches. However, there is no doubt that Torontonians consider public libraries too important to mess with. While the city's library system was and still is considered inviolable, another important community amenity wasn't so lucky in being able to duck closure.

This happened in 1867 when the city's only hospital at the time, the Toronto General, was forced to close its doors for nearly a year after money to run the facility ran out.

At the time, one of the all-too-few sources of income for these services was attained through grants from the city. So with Toronto facing financial problems, all of the grants were cut back or eliminated altogether. And with the newly established Province of Ontario still trying to find its way, grant money was not yet flowing from that source. Bills for medicine, food, medical staff, and repairs to the relatively new building on Gerrard Street were outstanding, and this ultimately forced the hospital to close its doors.

The city of some 50,000 residents went without this important medical facility until sufficient money was found to allow the Toronto General to reopen on August 3, 1868. The TGH has remained in business ever since.

August 7, 2011

City Streets Go Electric

As the young fellow said to a concerned Esther Smith (Judy Garland) as she hesitated boarding the streetcar that would take her and her friends (including John Truitt if he ever showed up) to Huntington Lake, "Tide, time, and trolley wait for no man."

— from the 1944 movie musical *Meet Me in St. Louis*

That young fellow could have uttered the same phrase to her in Toronto on August 15, 1892, the day that our city's first electric streetcar entered service. That historic car operated on the "Church" route that connected the old Union Station, opposite the foot of today's University Avenue, with South Drive in Rosedale using tracks that ran along Front, Church, Bloor, and Sherbourne streets.

To be historically accurate, Torontonians had been served by streetcars as far back as 1861 when an American company introduced citizens to a fleet of horse-drawn cars that ran on steel wheels and operated over steel rails. These "state-of-the-art" vehicles replaced the stagecoach service that had been run by local carpenter and part-time undertaker Henry Burt Williams. Unlike the more modern steel-wheeled vehicles, Mr. Williams's coaches kicked up clouds of dust as they made their way between the St. Lawrence Market and the suburban terminal just north of the Yonge and Bloor intersection.

There's little doubt that the city's 45,000 citizens were glad to see the end of those stagecoaches and enthusiastically endorsed Toronto city council's decision to award the American company the exclusive right to look after the city's transportation needs for the next thirty years.

But as improved as the quality of ride may have become, those horses were still a problem for a variety of reasons — expense, disease, and sanitation, to name just three.

Just like Toronto, cities all over the world were experiencing similar problems brought on by their own horse-drawn equipment. It wasn't long before the newest wonder of the age, electricity, was being adapted for use as a source of motive power. In fact, one of the first uses of an electric motor to power a vehicle operating on steel rails was pioneered at the Toronto Industrial Exhibition (now the CNE) in 1883. Two years later,

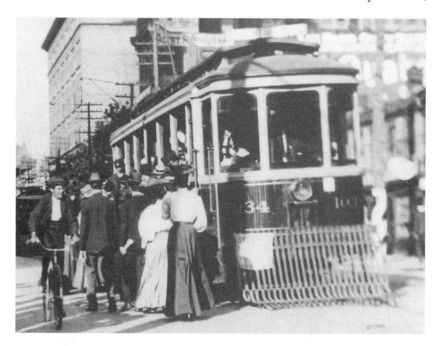

In this early 1900 photo, a cyclist rides by passengers waiting to board one of the early electric streetcars at the corner of Queen and James streets. Don't know if that manoeuvre was against the law back then, but it sure is now. The Robert Simpson store at the southwest corner of Yonge and Queen is visible in the background. Note the "cowcatcher" at the front of the vehicle.

the experiment had been perfected thanks in part to the use of a "trolley pole" that had been installed on top of the car. It permitted a constant supply of the necessary electrical current to be obtained from an overhead wire — a solution that was safer than other methods that had been tried by other cities. As it turned out, this now familiar trolley pole was a world first.

With the Toronto Street Railway's thirty-year charter coming to an end (and after a brief attempt by the municipality to operate the system on its own), a new company, the Toronto Railway Company, entered the picture. It, too, was given a thirty-year franchise. Included in the terms of this new contract was a requirement that the city's existing horse-powered system be converted to electric operations within two years. The company complied, and on August 15, 1892, Toronto's first electric streetcar went into service. Exactly two years and two weeks later, the last of the horse-drawn cars trotted into the history books.

Ever since that first electric vehicle glided up and down those city streets, the streetcar has been with us, and in spite of Mayor Rob Ford's efforts, I predict they will still be with us well into the future.

August 14, 2011

The vehicle in this photo is typical of those first electric streetcars. The operating crew consisted of a motorman and a conductor.

Gateway to Fun and Games

From the time the very first edition of what we know today as the Canadian National Exhibition opened to the public on Tuesday, September 2, 1879, the most important entrance into the sprawling grounds was located on the east side of Dufferin Street, just a short distance south of what was then a railway level crossing. Visitors paid their twenty-five-cent admission fee and entered the Toronto Industrial Exhibition (the original name of the fair and one it retained officially until 1912, although the term CNE was used as early as 1904) through a series of covered walkways. In 1895, a rather nondescript gateway was erected straddling the street, but it wasn't until 1910 that an impressive ceremonial gate was erected right at the foot of Dufferin. It was replaced by the present arch in 1956.

During the fair's earliest years, horse-drawn streetcars operated by the privately owned Toronto Street Railway Company carried Exhibition-bound visitors along King Street West, with the rest of the trip to the grounds having to be made on foot down Strachan or Dufferin Street. In 1892, the new electric streetcars of the Toronto Railway Company conveyed visitors along King and down Dufferin to a new loop laid out to serve the west end of the fairgrounds. It wasn't until 1916 that the company got permission to serve the east end of the CNE by operating cars from Bathurst Street to a loop near the northeast corner of the

Incorporated in this newspaper ad dated June 20, 1927, is a statement announcing that the name of the new eastern entranceway to the Canadian National Exhibition grounds would henceforth be known as the Diamond Jubilee of Confederation Arch. Within a few weeks the name was officially changed to the Princes' Gates.

grounds. The final routing was a compromise, with tracks laid on a right-of-way skirting the north side of Fort York. Initial attempts to operate cars right through the middle of the fort were thwarted, even though the company had suggested that such a route would be, to use today's vernacular, "good for tourism."

The imposing Princes' Gates forms a perfect backdrop for the start of this car rally. Note the long demolished eleven-storey Shell Oil Tower visible in the background. Erected in 1955, it was renamed the Bulova Tower in 1973 and demolished thirteen years later. The temperature shown on the readout is 62° Fahrenheit.

With all the activities and buildings concentrated at the west end of the grounds, it would be another eleven years before the east end of the CNE grounds started to be developed. To emphasize the impending addition of the vast Electrical and Engineering Building (opened in 1928, demolished in the early 1970s, and now the site of the Direct Energy Centre) and the sprawling Automotive Building (opened in 1929 and renamed the Allstream Centre in 2009) CNE officials decided to erect an imposing ceremonial entrance. In honour of the country's sixtieth anniversary of attaining nationhood, the original name of this new structure was to be the Diamond Jubilee of Confederation Arch. When it was announced that the princes, Edward and George, sons of the reigning British monarchs King George V and Queen Mary, would attend the 1927 edition of the fair and had agreed to dedicate the arch, the rather wordy title was changed to the more concise Princes' Gates.

August 21, 2011

Commuters of Yesteryear

As our city lurches forward with a variety of plans to build new transit facilities, either in the form of expensive subways or new streetcar and LRT lines, it's interesting to look back at how the commuters of yesterday got around town. Or in the case of thousands living north of the city, how they got in and out of the big city.

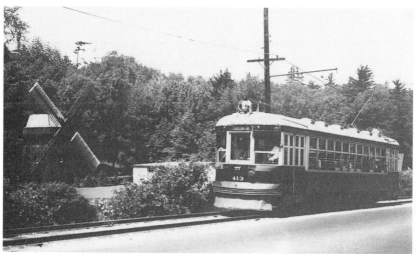

Courtesy of Bill Hood Collection.

The TTC operated streetcars similar to the number 413, seen here on the North Yonge radial line that ran between the Toronto City Limits (north end of the Hogg's Hollow hill) and Richmond Hill. This popular commuter service ended in 1948.

Two North Yonge Railway cars pause in Willowdale on their way north to Richmond Hill, circa 1941.

A similar view today looks south on Yonge Street just south of Finch Avenue.

While the earliest forms of travel featured slow and uncomfortable horse-drawn stage coaches, a major improvement arrived in 1885 with the introduction of electric streetcars on Yonge Street, north of the growing city. These vehicles initially served the folks living in the small country communities located between the Canadian Pacific Railway crossing north of Davenport Road and the concession road that had come to be known as Eglinton Avenue.

Over the years this pioneer route reached farther and farther north, eventually giving commuters in Bedford Park, York Mills (Hogg's Hollow), Lansing, Willowdale, Finches Corners, Newtonbrook, Steele's Corners, Thornhill, Richmond Hill, Aurora, Newmarket, Jackson's Point, and Sutton a quick, economical (and with the vehicles being electrically powered, and to use a modern-day term, environmentally friendly) connection with all the things the big city to the south had to offer. As well as a ride home.

This early commuter line was known as the Metropolitan Division of the privately owned Toronto and York Radial Railway (the term *radial* described a series of electric streetcar lines that radiated out from the city to the east, west, and north). The "Metropolitan's" end-of-the-line terminal opened in 1909 and was located in a building that still stands at the northeast corner of Dalton Road and High Street in Sutton, Ontario (at least it did when I last looked).

For the next twenty-one years the line, by then operated by the recently organized and municipally controlled Toronto Transportation Commission, was an important catalyst in the growth of numerous communities that had sprouted up on Yonge Street north of the city. However, it wasn't long before the TTC, tired of financing a route that operated for much of its length outside the City of Toronto, literally pulled the plug. On March 16, 1930, gasoline buses replaced streetcars on the route.

But that wasn't the end of the radials on Yonge. Just four months later, Richmond Hill and York Township officials got together and agreed to look after the money problems. On July 17, 1930, an abbreviated route between the Toronto City Limits and the Town of Richmond Hill was back in business.

However, a new threat stood in the way of the line's future — the province was running out of electricity. A huge growth in industry following the end of the Second World War and a failure to build any new power plants to supply them resulted in major power shortages at the time. To help alleviate the situation, it was agreed that the north Yonge radial cars would be replaced by gasoline buses (as were the streetcars on Spadina Avenue downtown). They also agreed that once the power concerns had been rectified the north Yonge radials would return. But they wouldn't, and at 4:30 in the morning on October 10, 1948, the Yonge radials on Canada's first radial streetcar line ceased operation.

Noronic's *Last Voyage*

The sun was just beginning to set on Friday, September 16, 1949, as Canada Steamship Lines' popular passenger vessel SS *Noronic* entered Toronto Harbour. Known by inland mariners as the "Queen of the Lakes" — a title bestowed on her after thirty-five years of faithful service — *Noronic* was on the second day of a special season-ending seven-day cruise that would take passengers from Detroit to the 1,000 Islands and back. Along the way she had stopped at Cleveland to pick up the last group of travellers, a number that would bring the ship's passenger complement up to 524, all American. The crew numbered 171, all Canadian.

Following a highly anticipated trip through the Welland Canal, *Noronic* had sailed out into Lake Ontario and on to Toronto for an overnight stay where the ship would be berthed alongside the company dock located just steps from the foot of Yonge Street.

At approximately 2:30 in the morning, as the vessel, its passengers, and most of her crew slept, a fire broke out in a small linen closet located near the ship's lounge. One of the passengers, unable to sleep and having spent some time up on deck, was making his way back to his stateroom. On the way, he noticed a wisp of smoke creeping out under the door of the locked closet. He immediately tried to locate a crew member in the hope that the two could extinguish the flames or at least raise the alarm.

Happier times: Under a clear blue sky in June 1937, two of Canada Steamship Lines' most popular passenger vessels, SS *Cayuga* (left) and SS *Noronic*, are seen moored in the CSL slip at the foot of Yonge Street. A dozen years later, flames would devour *Noronic*.

This photo conveys some idea of the scope of the conflagration that roared through *Noronic* in the early hours of September 17, 1949.

Toronto Harbour Commission/Toronto Port Authority Archives.

But it was already too late. Within what seemed like mere seconds, flames burst through the closet door and leapt out into the passageway, setting the ship's highly varnished wood trim, highly flammable carpets, and numerous coats of paint alight. It's difficult to believe in this day and age, when fire prevention and detection is of such importance, that it was in those first few minutes after the fire had first been detected that *Noronic's* fate was sealed.

Despite the efforts of city firemen, police officers, and a number of ordinary citizens, by the time the fire had been brought under control nearly three hours later, a total of 118 passengers had lost their lives, making the disaster the worst in our city's history. Of those 118, a total of fourteen unfortunates were never identified, their remains resting forever in a special plot in Mt. Pleasant Cemetery.

All the victims were passengers, a fact that wasn't overlooked as officials investigated how such a tragedy could happen. Where had the crew members been? And where was the ship's master, Captain Taylor, through it all?

As fate would have it, there would be one member of *Noronic's* crew added to the death toll. Louisa Dustin, the ship's fifty-two-year-old paymaster, had suffered extensive burns and been treated at Toronto General Hospital. She was subsequently relocated to a hospital in her hometown of Sarnia, but passed away there on October 9. *Noronic's* death toll was now 119, and Louisa was the only Canadian victim.

Several weeks later the ship's charred shell was towed to Hamilton to be scrapped.

There's much more to this sad story, certainly far more than can be accommodated in my column. One of the best and most comprehensive articles about the tragedy can be found online at *www.lostliners.com/ Peril/noronic.html.*

September 18, 2011

Gas Shortage Sparks Innovation

With the outbreak of the Second World War, oil and gasoline soon became scarce commodities. It wasn't long before travel by automobile and trucks (except for certain priority purposes — fire trucks, police vehicles, doctors' cars, etc.) all but vanished from city streets.

It was relatively easy (if not convenient) for members of the public to switch to public transit. Here in Toronto, the Toronto Transportation Commission did yeoman service, carrying unprecedented numbers of passengers to and from work on its hundreds of streetcars and buses. However, the decreasing availability of gasoline for the hundreds of delivery vehicles roaming Toronto streets soon became particularly acute. Some companies, such as those that provided home delivery (remember that?) of dairy and bakery products and even blocks of ice for the household ice box (remember those?) reverted back to the way most started in business; that is, by using real horse power.

One major Toronto enterprise, the iconic department store giant Simpson's (which had started out as the Robert Simpson Co. at the corner of Yonge and Queen streets in 1872) brought back some of its horses, but eventually decided to experiment with what officials thought was an even better idea.

Retrieving one of the gasoline-powered delivery trucks from its fleet, the vehicle was retrofitted with what can only be described as a modified barbecue that was affixed to the back of the vehicle. The idea was to substitute gas generated by the burning of plain, ordinary charcoal, which, because of the local abundance of forest products, would continue to be in plentiful supply. The gas generated was filtered through a damp pad before being fed into the truck's regular motor. It was found that an often cantankerous carburetor was unnecessary.

The only thing visible externally that distinguished this vehicle from all the others in the Simpson fleet was a large metal hopper used to hold the charcoal. This could be seen hanging on the back of the truck. A water-fed cooler was also necessary to keep the internal burner from overheating.

Initial tests done by the company mechanics revealed that by burning seventy pounds of charcoal, which cost roughly $3.50 (today charcoal sells for just over one dollar a pound), the equivalent of ten gallons of gasoline, a normal day's supply, was generated. And the truck could travel at forty miles per hour. It was also determined that the total cost of assembling and installing the equipment, which was built by the Dominion Bridge Company in Vancouver, was approximated $500.

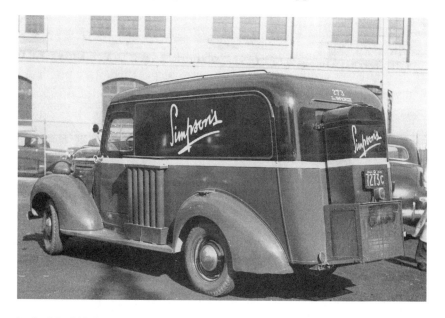

In the fall of 1943, and with gasoline being rationed because of the war, management at the Simpson's department store experimented with charcoal as a replacement fuel for their delivery vehicles.

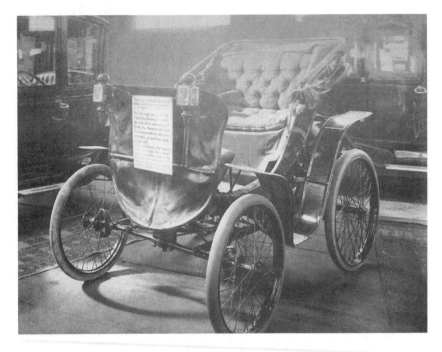

In 1893, Torontonians were amazed when they saw lawyer/inventor Fred Fetherstonhaugh zipping around town in his electric "horseless carriage," pictured here.

While the charcoal-powered delivery truck looked as if it would be a good alternative to the gasoline-powered vehicles, there were problems, many of which had already been determined by a series of similar experiments undertaken in Europe and Asia years earlier when similar oil shortages plagued nations there.

For instance, it took some time to get the burners lit and then generate enough charcoal gas to simply start the motor. And all the while there was the continual generation of huge amounts of deadly carbon monoxide gas, a by-product that was not a good thing to have permeating a closed garage.

All in all, at a time when the lifeblood of the delivery business was in such short supply (and getting worse) it was obviously important to at least try out some alternate fuels. It's just that charcoal wasn't going to do the trick, especially without a lot of effort to remedy its side effects. The ultimate fate of the Simpson project is unknown, though it's a good bet it was simply abandoned after the initial public viewing.

With the return of peace in 1945, petroleum products became abundant once more and the search for alternate fuels took a back seat. Until the next time oil became scarce and the search was on once more.

Any story about the search for alternate fuels to power the automobile would be incomplete without mentioning, however briefly, the innovative work done by local lawyer/inventor Frederick Barnard Fetherstonhaugh. Combining his talents with those of local electrician William Still, by 1893 the pair had created a highly successful electrically-powered automobile that was in several respects similar to today's revolutionary all-electric cars such as Nissan's *Leaf* and the Tesla *Roadster* and *Model S*. But that's another story for another column.

September 25, 2011

Air Museum Home Up in the Air

Showing an amazing lack of public relations savvy, officials of the sprawling urban recreational area called Downsview Park recently and arbitrarily decided that the doors of the fourteen-year-old volunteer-driven Canadian Air and Space Museum located in one of the park's largest buildings would be closed. And to emphasize that the officials meant business, they ordered the locks and keys to the museum be changed, immediately. Suddenly the future of the museum, as well as the safety of its precious artifacts, was very much in doubt.

As this story is being written, rumours persist that negotiations are underway to ensure the museum's future. Therefore, so as not to upset that apple cart, let me simply pass on some information that will help convince the reader that the building in which the museum was located must be part of any "rescue" program. First though, a brief preface.

The de Havilland Aircraft Company arrived in Canada in 1928 and set up a small factory adjacent to the pioneer De Lesseps Airfield on today's Trethewey Drive. It was here that their Moth biplanes, which had arrived in crates from the company's plant in England, were assembled by hand and sold to an eager public. Business was brisk, and before long a larger facility was needed. In 1929 the company purchased sixty acres of farmland not far from the two dirt concession roads we now know as Sheppard and Dufferin.

Over the next few years a number of buildings and hangars were constructed to provide space for the manufacture of de Havilland products requested for both the military and for a number of emerging flying clubs. With the outbreak of the Second World War, the original 1929 building was greatly enlarged, and it was in this mammoth new building that Canadian aviation history was made as the company designed and turned out more than 7,500 civilian and military aircraft that were and continue to be flown in more than one hundred countries worldwide. Planes with names like Moth, Mosquito, Chipmunk, Beaver, Otter, and Caribou have become synonymous with de Havilland, Downsview, and Canada.

After the war, the RCAF occupied the building for a time. It was followed by a variety of enterprises that helped thrust Canada into the space age, such as the assembly and testing of the Alouette, the world's first scientific space satellite. It was also in this building that de Havilland's Special Products Division was formed. It in time evolved into SPAR Aerospace, creators of the Canadarm.

In spite of the public's condemnation of the action, in late 2011 the landlords forced the closure of the Canadian Air and Space Museum at Downsview Park. It is hoped that this popular and important museum

Courtesy of Ken Greenbury.

Sunday Sun reader (and fellow member of the Thornhill Cruisers Car Club) Ken Greenbury recently forwarded this interesting photo from the family scrapbook. Ken's father, Arthur (far right), poses with his colleagues in front of one of the more than 1,100 Mosquito aircraft built by de Havilland in its Downsview, Ontario, factory.

will reopen in a new location, perhaps at Toronto Pearson International Airport, in the near future.

To learn more about the uncertain future of the Canadian Air and Space Museum and 65 Carl Hall Road please visit *www.casmuseum.org*.

October 2, 2011

* This important message related to the future of the Canadian Air and Space Museum was recently posted on the organization's website:

> *The Canadian Air & Space Museum is pleased to confirm discussions with the Greater Toronto Airports Authority (GTAA) regarding the potential opening of a revitalized Museum in an outstanding new location which will allow for vastly improved access for residents and visitors to the Greater Toronto Area.*
>
> *The Greater Toronto Airport Authority, along with several airport based private businesses, including Flight Solutions and Services, Partner Jet, UYJ Air, and MxAerospace are together providing interim storage of the Museum's important artifacts and archival material while potential development opportunities within the Greater Toronto Airport Authority's site are explored.*
>
> *No binding commitments have been made at this time. However, the Museum Trustees and the GTAA are evaluating opportunities to preserve and present Toronto's aviation past, which includes watershed achievements at both the Malton and Downsview airports. All the parties share a belief that Toronto's many aviation and space contributions to Canada's rich history should be presented in innovative and exciting ways for the enjoyment and educational benefit of future generations.*
>
> *Ian A. McDougall*
> *Chairman for the Board of Directors*
> *Canadian Air & Space Museum*

Barker Finally Gets His Due

Several years ago, I was busily compiling material for a book on the history of Mount Pleasant Cemetery, a publication that would include stories about as many of the people who now call Mount Pleasant "home" as I could fit in while still keeping the price within reason. With more than two hundred thousand individuals to choose from, it wasn't difficult to fill the book with stories about the two survivors of the *Titanic* sinking, or the nine victims of the deadly hurricane called Hazel that devastated parts of southern Ontario in 1954, or the schoolteacher who entered a songwriting contest with a tune that went on to become Canada's unofficial national anthem. However, I couldn't find one of the cemetery's "residents" who I wanted to include. His name was William George Barker. And just why did I want to include him? The answer to that question is simple: Barker continues to be regarded as Canada's most decorated war hero and one of our country's very few Victoria Cross recipients. He just had to be in the book.

William George Barker was born on November 3, 1894, on the family farm near Dauphin, Manitoba. Following the outbreak of the Great War, Barker joined the 1st Canadian Mounted Rifles. Soon after his arrival in England, he transferred to the Royal Flying Corps, where he pursued his love of the wonder of the age (as rickety as they may have been) — airplanes.

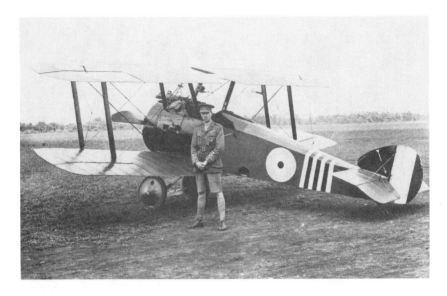

William Barker, VC, is recognized as the most decorated war hero in the history of Canada, the British Empire, and the Commonwealth of Nations. Here he poses with one of his favourite aircraft, a Sopwith Camel.

For the duration of the war he served on both the Western and Italian fronts. By the end of the war, the young Canadian had been credited with destroying fifty enemy aircraft. Barker returned home with a badly wounded body and a chest full of medals, which included the Victoria Cross, a decoration that was first introduced in 1856 "for valour in the face of the enemy." Historically, fewer than one hundred Canadians have ever received this highly coveted award.

Barker, in partnership with another Canadian war hero and VC recipient, Billy Bishop, went on to establish the country's first commercial airline. Unfortunately, it was his love of aviation that would end Barker's life. He died on March 12, 1930, when a new aircraft he was demonstrating for officials of the Department of Defence crashed at Ottawa's Rockcliffe Airport.

So I was determined to find Barker's final resting place. Articles in all the local newspapers described his funeral, complete with full military honours, which took place at Mount Pleasant Cemetery a few days after the accident. But none of those articles mentioned the location of Barker's final resting place. I couldn't help but think that if he had been an American there'd be all kinds of signs pointing the way to the grave site and quite possibly a souvenir stand nearby. But there was nothing. A closer search of the cemetery records led me to the mausoleum, but there were no clues to tell me just where inside that beautiful building I would find our hero.

Finally, after some additional searching, I discovered that his name wasn't visible on any of the mausoleum's many rooms or crypts because he had been interred with his wife's family. Her maiden name was Smith; finally, a clue.

And sure enough, a closer inspection of a location described as Smith, Room B, Crypt B led me to him.

Although William Barker VC had been virtually forgotten for more than eight decades, descendents recently agreed it was time that this Canadian hero was recognized. And so, on September 13, 2011, Lieutenant Governor David Onley unveiled a commemorative plaque and a monument in the shape of a biplane's propeller at the entrance to Barker's final resting place in the Mount Pleasant Cemetery Mausoleum.

October 9, 2011

On September 13, 2011, distinctive memorials in the form of a propeller along with a descriptive plaque were unveiled in front of the mausoleum in Mount Pleasant Cemetery where Barker VC was entombed more than eighty years earlier.

The Street Name Game

O ne of the most interesting ways to learn about a community's history is to study the origins of its various street names. To be sure, many of them are purely descriptive, such as Maple, Elm, or Centre, or Toronto's Bayview (a view of the bay) and Broadview (a broad view of downtown over the Riverdale Flats). Other city streets recall battles (Sorauren, Pretoria), members of the royalty and their friends (King for King George III, Yonge for one of his cabinet ministers, Sir George Yonge), early settlers' hometowns (Doncaster, Islington), or other prominent city settlers and visitors from the past (McCowan, Kipling).

Every once in a while a street name is changed or altered (Awde became Croatia, lower Peter became Blue Jays Way, north Jarvis became Ted Rogers Way). Thankfully, such changes are infrequent; however, back in the 1930s there was a plan put forward to change the name of Carlton Street to College Street East. This idea came about in early 1931 as the city and the TTC were planning to eliminate the jog that for years had made it necessary for vehicular and streetcar traffic heading west on Carlton or east on College to make sharp turns on and off Yonge Street, because at the time College and Carlton were totally separate streets.

To make Carlton and College one continuous thoroughfare (and provide employment for Depression-weary workers) several buildings

In this June 1931 photo from the TTC Archives, crews work on laying streetcar tracks along a newly constructed right-of-way built to eliminate the jog at the old and very difficult College–Yonge–Carlton intersection. The old tracks to the extreme left of the picture connected Carlton Street with Yonge several hundred yards south of the present realigned intersection. The new Eaton's College Street store (now College Park) is in the background.

Photo by Yarmila Filey.

A similar view looks west along Carlton Street from just west of Church. Note that the castellated roof on the old building that still stands at the northwest corner of Yonge and College appears in both photos.

on the east side of Yonge were demolished and a slight curve laid out allowing Carlton to run into Yonge opposite College.

Once the two streets became one continuous thoroughfare in early July 1931, city officials believed that one name would make things easier for drivers. And to differentiate them the names College Street East and College Street West would be used. They obviously didn't count on an uproar from the history buffs of the day, but when the dust settled it was decided that the original names would be kept.

So who was this Carlton person anyway?

Guy Carelton Wood (note the correct spelling of Carelton) was a prominent city businessman and the brother of Ann McGill, who was the wife of the Bishop John Strachan, arguably the most important clergyman during the city's formative years. When the McGill family donated land in the vicinity of today's Maple Leaf Gardens (am I allowed to use that name?) to the city, Mrs. McGill requested that her brother's middle name be recognized in the title of any new street that was cut through the property.

And College Street? It was originally known as the Yonge Street Avenue and led east from the old King's College (1827–50), a building that was located where the Ontario Legislature Buildings now stand. That rather confusing street name was changed to the present College Street about the same time King's College took up a new site farther to the west along with a new name — the University of Toronto.

October 16, 2011

Toronto's Steamy Past

I'm sure some of my readers will remember with great fondness spring, summer, or fall trips on the SS *Assiniboia* or SS *Keewatin*, two of the most popular passenger boats to navigate the waters of Georgian Bay and Lake Superior. The two were built for the Canadian Pacific Railway at the Fairfield Company Shipbuilding Yard in Govan, Scotland, in 1907. Following an uneventful crossing of the Atlantic, the pair, being too large for the existing St. Lawrence and Welland Canals, were cut in half and towed to a Buffalo, New York shipyard, where they were reassembled.

The following year saw the two 350-foot-long vessels, each with a passenger capacity of nearly three hundred, enter the lucrative passenger and freight service between Owen Sound and Port Arthur/Fort William (renamed Thunder Bay in 1970).

In the ship's early days the majority of passengers were recent immigrants from Europe seeking a fresh start somewhere, anywhere in western Canada, and who had made their way to the CPR's Owen Sound dock by train from Toronto. The return trip from the lakehead ports saw the vessels fully loaded with huge quantities of grain and lumber. In 1912, the eastern terminal for the lake boats (*Assiniboia*, *Keewatin*, and several other smaller vessels) was relocated to a newly laid out town to be known as Port McNicoll, so named to honour David McNicoll, CPR's

Courtesy of Scott Garrett.

The CPR passenger steamer SS *Keewatin* waits at its new Port McNicoll dock for passengers who have just arrived on the special "Boat Train" from Toronto, 1912.

In 1967, two years after SS *Keewatin* ended scheduled passenger service between Port McNicoll and the lakehead destinations of Port Arthur and Fort William (renamed Thunder Bay in 1970), the historic vessel was rescued from the wreckers and put on display in Douglas, Michigan.

This souvenir postcard shows the *SS Keewatin*, circa 1930.

vice-president and general manager of the day. It was there that spacious passenger facilities (complete with beautifully landscaped gardens) and huge storage elevators were built. "The Port" (as the place eventually became known locally) also replaced Owen Sound as the terminus of the extremely popular "Boat Trains," which carried passengers by the thousands north from Toronto's Union Station.

While the SS *Assiniboia* no longer exists (having been destroyed by fire four years after she retired from service and while on the way to being converted into a floating restaurant) her running mate, the SS *Keewatin*, experienced a far happier fate — the ship has been home to a floating museum in the harbour at Douglas, Michigan, for the past forty-four years.

Now here's where the story gets particularly interesting. Lengthy negotiations with the American owner of SS *Keewatin* have resulted in a plan to return the historic vessel (recognized as the oldest Edwardian-era passenger boat in the world) to Port McNicoll, where she will be a major feature of a proposed $1.7-billion redevelopment of "The Port." The move from Douglas, Michigan, to Port McNicoll is scheduled for the spring of 2012.

October 23, 2011

* On June 23, 2012, SS *Keewatin* returned to Port McNicoll where the historic vessel awaits her future as a floating museum. Details and updates can be found at *www.sskeewatin.com*.

"Kipling's Road to Woodbridge"

One day I was chatting with a group of people about books and whether any of us really believed that the new eReaders would eventually replace real books. We began discussing various authors, and suddenly, out of the blue, someone asked me if I liked Kipling. I replied that I really didn't know since I have never kippled.

Now, the reason I present my readers this very old joke is to give me a chance to offer my suggestion as to why one of the city's busiest west end thoroughfares is named in honour of the famous English author, Mr. Rudyard Kipling. Nice segue, eh?

When early surveyors began laying out what were initially nothing more than dirt pathways through the Township of Etobicoke's forests and meadows, little thought was given to adding a name to each. In fact, many years would pass before the first few roads would get any name at all. The vast majority existed for decades as simply numbered concessions or side roads. There were two notable exceptions, the Lakeshore Road and the Dundas Highway, the former so named because of its location beside the Lake Ontario shoreline and the latter because it was a continuation of an existing street in the Town of York (a community that would be renamed Toronto in 1834), one that the province's first lieutenant governor, John Graves Simcoe, had named to honour Sir Henry Dundas, the Secretary of State in King George III's cabinet. Simcoe intended that this road

(which is one year older than Yonge Street) would connect the existing provincial capital at York with his intended site for a new, more easily defensible capital to be established where London, Ontario, is today.

Rudyard Kipling (1865–1936), poet, novelist, and recipient of the 1907 Nobel Prize in Literature.

While there were at least two named streets in the township, there were dozens without names. One of the north–south roads was the one we know today as Kipling Avenue. Unfortunately, as with many street names back then, no one gave any thought to recording why a certain name was selected. This fact drives history buffs crazy. In the case of Kipling Avenue, we have to wonder why this dusty, often muddy rural pathway would be given a name that recognized one of the best-known individuals of the late eighteenth/early nineteenth century. And so we are left to speculate. So let me do just that.

In 1907, Rudyard Kipling was awarded the Nobel Prize in Literature. Late that same year, he and his wife toured the United States and Canada, making a stop here in Toronto on October 17. His speaking engagement at McConkey's Assembly Rooms (31 King Street West) drew a packed house, with the 750 available tickets selling out in just a few hours. When officials of the Woodbridge Fair learned of Kipling's impending visit, they quickly decided to request this (to use a modern-day term) "superstar" officiate at the opening of its 1907 edition. And how would he get to the fairgrounds from the four-year-old King Edward Hotel on King Street where he was staying? Part of the trip (no doubt by the hotel's special tally-ho coach) would take him via one of the township's unnamed north–south roads that someone might have taken the liberty of describing as "Kipling's road to Woodbridge." This possibility is made even more plausible by the fact that the fairground is located on Kipling Avenue, a continuation of that Etobicoke thoroughfare through Woodbridge.

Unfortunately, Kipling declined the offer to open the fair, citing conflicting personal business matters. Nevertheless, I'll stick by my theory until someone comes up with something better.

October 30, 2011

Cop Shops, Old and New

Police stations have certainly come a long way from those wood or brick buildings that were in use back in the "good old days." A perfect example of how things have progressed is the Toronto Police Service's gleaming new 11 Division at 2054 Davenport Road. It was officially opened on October 28, 2011, replacing an earlier 1950s-era 11 Division building at 209 Mavety Street in "The Junction." Thanks to the skills of the Stantec Architecture team, the officers of 11 Division now find themselves in a new state-of-the-art home that integrates green-roof utilization, a geothermal energy system, highly efficient use and reuse of water, and an extensive recycling system.

But as modern as this new station would turn out to be, every individual involved in the project agreed that it was essential that some recognizable heritage feature of the community be incorporated into the new structure. And since the new building would be erected on the footprint of the historic 1913 Carleton Village Public School, the obvious choice was to incorporate a significant segment of the old school's familiar south façade as well as several of the rooms in which many members of the community spent their earliest school years.

The name of the old school prompts the question: Where and what was this village called Carleton, and did the person who named it fail spelling? Greg McKinnon, the Toronto District School Board's always helpful archivist, advises that during the late 1800s a small village called Carleton grew up in and around the crossroads we now know today as St. Clair and Old Weston Road. It's quite likely that the community was named in honour of Sir Guy Carleton, governor general of British North America (1786–96) and the chief administrator during the years our province and city were first established (1791 and 1793 respectively).

The Court Street station in downtown Toronto opened in 1874 and for many years was used by both the police and fire departments. The unusual building was demolished soon after it closed as a police station in 1960.

The Town of East Toronto was annexed by the City of Toronto in 1908. Pictured here is one of the community's original police stations, which was still in use three years after annexation.

Toronto Police Service's impressive new 11 Division on Davenport Road, just east of Old Weston Road, was officially opened on October 28, 2011. The building incorporates a portion of the old Carleton Village Public School.

Two other interesting features of the 11 Division neighbourhood are the names of nearby thoroughfares. Ford Street runs just to the west, while across Davenport Road is a thoroughfare named Miller. Needless to say, neither recognizes our two most recent mayors, but were instead named for two early community businessmen.

November 13, 2011

Road Pioneers of the Past

Anyone who thinks that traffic congestion caused by pavement and bridge construction followed by the inevitable repairing and replacement of same is something new can take comfort in the fact that traffic congestion actually originated the day after Lieutenant Governor John Graves Simcoe's Queen's Rangers began construction of the Town of York's first "inter-city" highway more than two centuries ago. That project was started in 1798 and was intended to connect Simcoe's young provincial capital (to be renamed Toronto in 1834) with "the head of the lake," a destination we know today as Hamilton.

Interestingly, as the years went by little was done to improve that original route along the Lake Ontario shoreline. This was partly because farmers with property that fronted on Lake Ontario were reluctant to allow the widening of the old lakeshore right-of-way. With no major improvements being planned, travellers looked inland and quickly discovered that the Middle Road (the route that would be followed by the QEW years later) and the pioneer Dundas Highway, a few miles farther to the north, had fewer hills and ravines. These two roads soon became the much preferred way to get between Hamilton and Toronto.

However, by the early 1910s the greatly increased number of automobiles and trucks using the Middle Road and Dundas Highway forced the various levels of local government to come up with plans for an improved connection between the two burgeoning Ontario cities. That plan resulted in the construction of a new thirty-six-mile-long thoroughfare to be known as the Toronto–Hamilton Highway. It would run between the Humber River in the east and the eastern outskirts of Hamilton in the west. The road surface would be poured concrete slabs and was described as being "the finest roadway of its kind on the continent." Unfortunately, freezing and thawing cycles each winter cracked the slabs and maintenance became extremely costly. Eventually, the concrete would be replaced with more durable asphalt paving.

Work on the new highway began on November 8, 1914, and while there was a war raging in Europe, it was assumed that the fighting would no doubt be over by the coming Christmas. But the war dragged on and soon men and materials became scarce. Politics also impeded construction, with municipal governments along the route unable to agree on such things as how wide the road should be through each community or just how much each jurisdiction should pay of the estimated $920,000 cost of the highway (needless to say, the project went way over budget,

Officials, including Ontario premier William Hearst, Toronto mayor Tommy Church, and Highway Commission chairman George Gooderham, celebrate the opening of the new Toronto–Hamilton Highway on November 24, 1917.

but the final figure seems to have been buried in the widely fluctuating wartime estimates). Closer to Toronto the presence of the Toronto and York Radial Railway tracks between Sunnyside and Port Credit had a major impact on the ultimate width and cost of the vehicle part of the highway. Just who was responsible for those added costs?

Historically, the new Toronto–Hamilton Highway was officially open on November 24, 1917, with great fanfare and a large complement of local and provincial politicians grasping the ceremonial ribbon. However, with the war hindering the availability of steel to build bridges over the Mimico, Etobicoke, and Bronte Creeks and over the Credit River, or to complete the approaches to those structures, it meant that many more months would pass before the route was truly complete.

November 20, 2011

In this undated photo we see crews pouring concrete slabs for the new Toronto–Hamilton Highway where it passes through Oakville. Concrete was susceptible to cracking under freeze-thaw conditions and was eventually replaced by asphalt.

House that Conn Smythe Built

It was on Wednesday, December 1, 2011, that Maple Leaf Gardens embarked on its new life as the home of Loblaws at Maple Leaf Gardens. This change occurred eighty years (less eighteen days) after the Maple Leafs hockey team played its first game in the new dream ice palace of team owner Connie Smythe. Though the outcome of that November 12, 1931, game was a less than happy one (the Chicago Black Hawks beat the Leafs 2–1), the Toronto team went on to win the 1931–32 Stanley Cup.

Originally planned for a waterfront location near the foot of Yonge Street, Smythe decided instead to build on a site on the north side of Carlton Street at the northwest corner of Church. This property had been presented to Smythe and his business associates at an extremely good price by the Eaton department store people. The location wasn't far from the company's proposed new main store, a building we now know as College Park. No doubt the proximity of the hockey arena to the new Eaton's store would be good for the department store's business.

The mammoth structure (for the time) was built in the incredibly short span of five months at a cost of nearly $1.5 million. Maple Leaf Gardens was built to replace the team's former home rink on Mutual Street, which had become too small to handle the increasing number of fans. The new structure would also provide accommodation for a variety of public shows and attractions which the city was ill-equipped to host.

Well on its way to becoming Toronto's newest icon, the roof of the new Maple Leaf Gardens could be seen for miles.

On September 21, 1931, Maple Leaf Gardens' president J.P. Bickell (right) assists Ontario's lieutenant governor, William D. Ross, with the dedication of the building's cornerstone. I wonder what they put in it.

Readers will no doubt recall the apprehension felt by many Torontonians when it was announced that following the February 13, 1999, NHL hockey game between the Toronto Maple Leafs and the Chicago Blackhawks (a game the Leafs would also lose 6–2) the hometown team would vacate the Gardens after nearly sixty-eight years worth of games in the "house that Smythe built." (Exactly one week later the Leafs played their first game in a new home, the Air Canada Centre. This time the result of that historic game would be more fitting, with a defeat of the Montreal Canadians in a 3–2 overtime victory.)

Many demanded that the Gardens be retained as a public skating rink, perhaps not realizing that the ultimate preservation of any federal, provincial, or municipally designated building can never be counted as a sure thing. The slated-for-demolition federally-designated de Havilland aircraft factory at Downsview Park that was subsequently reborn as the home of the Canadian Air and Space Museum is a perfect example of the futility of the nation's various preservation rules and regulations.

As a result of this unfortunate fact of life, it was not inconceivable that the beloved Gardens would simply be demolished and the site covered over with townhouses and condominium towers. To be sure, there'd be an historic plaque somewhere nearby.

It wasn't long after the new Maple Leaf Gardens opened in November 1931 that the building became the subject of the popular method of communications of the day — the souvenir postcard.

With the possibility of losing the Gardens, the announcement made two years ago by Loblaws officials that the company, along with Ryerson University, would retain and redevelop the iconic Maple Leaf Gardens was, to me at least, the only realistic answer to preventing what would have been the tragic loss of another city landmark.

November 27, 2011

* Since this column appeared, a new Loblaws store has opened (November 30, 2011) in the lower levels of the Gardens. On August 13, 2012, the new Mattamy Athletic Centre opened on the upper level.

Sunnyside Had Quite a Ride

It was near the end of the year in 1955 that Toronto's most popular fair-weather pleasure ground, a place known far and wide simply as "Sunnyside," was finally put out of its misery. Increasing traffic congestion and newer, more sophisticated ways for citizens and visitors to spend their leisure time had combined to doom the amusement park that had welcomed hundreds of thousands of pleasure-seekers from Victoria Day to Labour Day each year since it had opened back in 1922.

Built by the Toronto Harbour Commission (renamed the Toronto Port Authority in 1999) on a large parcel of land reclaimed from the old Humber Bay, this park was just one part of a master plan put forward in 1912 by the commission to improve the city's waterfront from the Humber River in the west almost as far east as the Scarborough Township boundary.

To increase the amount of land on which to build the new park, a modern traffic boulevard that would stretch from the Humber to the foot of Bathurst Street, a wooden boardwalk along the Lake Ontario shoreline, and a protective concrete break wall, it was agreed that a large area of the old Humber Bay would be filled in. To complete this monumental task, huge quantities of material dredged from the lake bottom would be used and "dressed" with clean topsoil transported to the waterfront from farms in Scarborough.

ROLLER-COASTER, AEROPLANE RIDE AND MERRY-GO-ROUND, SUNNYSIDE BEACH, TORONTO, ONT.

This rare picture postcard shows just a small area of Toronto's popular Sunnyside Amusement Park. Visible are the roller-coaster (a few of its cars went on to operate on the CNE's later lamented Flyer) and a popular Merry-Go-Round, one of two such rides. The other was called the Derby Racer.

The end of Sunnyside is near, as workers demolish the park's last few rides and buildings in late 1955. When this photo was taken, the Merry-Go-Round horses were on their way to the newly opened Disneyland in California, where they continue to prance today on King Arthur's Carousel.

Too bad no one thought to save the once familiar Sunnyside Beach sign that welcomed drivers arriving in Toronto via Lake Shore Boulevard over the old Humber River bridge.

In addition to a multitude of rides, there would also be games, food stands, restaurants, and a dance hall to be located in a building that began life as a boat-building factory.

During the Great Depression the park was a godsend. It was even more welcome during the Second World War, when gas and tires were strictly rationed. For most Torontonians, good old Sunnyside was a streetcar ride and a whole world away.

But with the return of peace, the park began to look old-fashioned in a city that was quickly modernizing. And with increased traffic congestion along the city's western waterfront, where the proposed cross-waterfront elevated highway (Gardiner) was still years in the future, the park was, quite simply, in the way.

With Sunnyside's future uncertain, no one was prepared to paint up or fix up. Then, in the fall of 1955, several fires of uncertain origin destroyed a couple of the park's old wooden buildings. Fearing something more serious, the Harbour Commission had the perfect excuse to shut the place down. A tender notice was placed in the local newspapers and after receiving only one response the contract was awarded to Brantford, Ontario's Kepic Brothers. The wrecking company purchased what was left of Toronto's favourite playground for the munificent sum of $355.

December 4, 2011

Great Snowstorm of '44

It's a Thursday afternoon in December, and as I sit here at my desk preparing this week's *Sunday Sun* column, I'm looking out the window at an unusually green, wet, and snow-free backyard. It's almost Christmas, for heaven's sake, and there's still no snow. So to make things at least seem a little more Christmas-like, I present the reader with a couple of photographs depicting the city the year there was just too much snow. In fact, although the local weather report for December 12, 1944, predicted "flurries" starting late in the day, by the time the storm petered out twenty hours later, almost 58 centimetres of the white stuff blanketed the city and most of the surrounding communities, with Hamilton receiving even more than Toronto (61 centimetres).

What made getting rid of this monstrous amount of snow even more difficult was the fact that the war in Europe had greatly reduced the availability of the manpower needed to clear the streets. That, combined with rationing of gasoline for mechanized equipment, meant that many of the side streets remained blocked for days. The main roads were eventually made passable, but only just.

Delivering coal to the thousands of houses with furnaces (like the one in Ralphie Parker's family home in the classic film *A Christmas Story*) was more than difficult, and those who didn't clear a path from the snow-choked street to the coal chute would simply have to go without.

Milk was delivered to the local fire hall, where it would be collected. But that solution soon led to a shortage of bottles, and dairies pleaded with customers to return them so that they'd have something in which to deliver the fresh milk. At least with today's modern containers, we'll have lots of milk next time we get two feet of snow!

December 18, 2011

Following the worst snowstorm in the city's history, people made their way to work the best they could, even if it meant climbing onto the back of a streetcar.

Flanked by a huge snowdrift, a pedestrian makes his way along King Street just west of Yonge Street in the aftermath of the storm of December 12–13, 1944.

Trip Down Gasoline Alley

In 1880, a group of sixteen businessmen with oil wells scattered throughout southwestern Ontario joined together to form a new business. They called their new enterprise the Imperial Oil Company.

Back then the main use for their crude oil, which was selling for 25 cents a gallon, was as a lubricant for farm machinery. It was also used to eliminate squeaky horse-drawn carriage wheels and axles. And as there was no use for one of crude's many by-products, something called "gasolene," it was simply drained into the local creeks, rivers, or swamps.

At least that was the situation until the new-fangled horseless carriages began showing up on city streets and country back roads. Suddenly there was a use for this former waste by-product. Initially the automobile's gas tank was filled with gasoline purchased from a local store using any container that could be found around the house or farm. Then, in 1907, Imperial Oil tried something new, opening an early version of the modern automobile service station in Vancouver. Before long these "gas" stations, operated by a multitude of oil companies, most with names now forgotten, began appearing in cities and towns all across the country.

One of the oldest service station sites in Toronto is the one operated by the Esso people at the southwest corner of Lake Shore Boulevard and Bathurst Street. Unfortunately, no one seems to know the exact date when the first "flivvers" drove up to the newly opened station's

This late 1920s photograph looks west from the southwest corner of Bathurst and Fleet streets. It shows the Imperial Oil gas station that is still in business on that corner, though now renamed Esso. Fleet Street was renamed Lake Shore Boulevard West in the early 1960s. Visible in the background on the right is the historic Queen's Wharf lighthouse.

A similar view today from the southwest corner of Bathurst Street and Lake Shore Boulevard.

pumps to fill up with twenty-five-cent-a-gallon gasoline. What we do know is that the land on which the station stands was reclaimed by the Toronto Harbour Commission by filling in the "old" and dangerous Western Channel. It was on this same land that the commission built the International Baseball League's most modern (for the day) stadium for the city's popular Maple Leaf baseball team. That structure opened in the spring of 1926, one year before the sprawling Loblaws warehouse and distinctive Crosse and Blackwell jams and pickles manufacturing plant opened on the northeast and southeast corners. My guess is that the Imperial (now Esso) gas station opened about the same time as those two structures.

Incidentally, close inspection of the old photo (in the background on the right side of photo) reveals the 1861 Queen's Wharf lighthouse standing in its original location just west of the foot of Bathurst Street, where it guided ships into Toronto Harbour from a position on the north side of the old Western Channel. As a result of extensive land-filling operations in the early 1920s, the lighthouse was left high and dry. Then, in an early example of the desire to preserve a few historic landmarks, the "ancient" structure was moved to its present location, several hundred metres to the west, where it continues to remind us of our waterfront history from its setting in the TTC's Lighthouse Loop.

December 26, 2011

Get Wind of This ...

There's been a great deal in the media recently about windmills (a.k.a. wind turbines) and whether they are as safe and as energy-efficient as some are suggesting. Hundreds of these structures can be found all over Canada, with the nation's second largest wind farm located on Wolfe Island, just south of the historic city of Kingston. Here in Toronto we have but one wind turbine. It is situated in Exhibition Place near the foot of Dufferin Street and is owned by an organization known as Windshare and the Toronto Renewable Energy Co-operative. This ninety-one-metre-high windmill began generating electricity on January 23, 2003.

While the concept of using the wind to generate electricity may have been new a decade ago, using wind off the lake certainly wasn't a new idea for the pioneers who developed one of Toronto's first industries.

What would eventually become the world-famous Gooderham and Worts distillery enterprise actually started off as a milling business. The origin of this business goes back to 1831, a full three years before the town of York was elevated to city status and renamed Toronto. Newcomers to the town, Messrs. Gooderham and Worts built a windmill that was used to power a large millstone that ground grain. This structure became one of the earliest landmarks on the young city's "skyline."

This windmill stood near the foot of Parliament Street and was a reproduction of the original Gooderham and Worts windmill located at the nearby G&W site.

As the milling business grew, additional grinding power was needed and the windmill's output was increased by adding a small steam engine. Eventually the old, and by then decrepit, windmill was pulled down altogether. Before long it became obvious to Gooderham and Worts that there was a great deal more money to be made by distilling the grain into drinkable product, and eventually G&W became one of the largest distillery operations in the world. It was proven that there wasn't nearly as much money in the dough.

Many years later a reproduction of that historic windmill was erected south of the Lake Shore Boulevard–Parliament Street intersection. But with the construction of the new elevated Cross-Waterfront Expressway (the Gardiner) in the mid-1950s, the structure was pulled down.

The original windmill served another rather interesting purpose. Its location, south and slightly west of today's Trinity and Mill street crossroads, was declared by the city surveyor as the east end of an imaginary line to be known, rather fittingly, as the "Windmill Line." The west end of this line was set at the site of the old French fort (Fort Toronto) that was, interestingly enough, just east of the other windmill I've been describing, the wind turbine that stands today in Exhibition Place.

One of North Yonge Railways high-speed streetcars rumbles by the windmill that had become a local landmark next to the York Springs factory. The streetcar operated between the City Limits and Richmond Hill from 1930 to 1948.

The purpose of the line was to delineate the southernmost limit of any wharves built out into Toronto Harbour. Without this reference point, wharves could stretch out as far as their owners wanted, thus giving them virtually unlimited loading and unloading space.

This O'Keefe's Ginger Ale newspaper ad appeared in July 1931. Water for this popular refreshment came from artesian wells on the west side of Yonge Street, halfway down the Hogg's Hollow hill.

There was one other windmill that became a landmark in Toronto. It was located on the northern outskirts of the city. However, unlike the waterfront structure, this one, on the west side of the Yonge Street hill as it descends into Hogg's Hollow, was only for show, a kind of advertising billboard. It was erected in 1931 by the O'Keefe beverage company next to its York Springs factory, where mineral water was drawn from artesian wells, bottled, and shipped to the city for use in the company's various beverages. This interesting structure disappeared in the mid-1950s to allow for the construction of the York Mills Garden Apartments.

January 29, 2012

Death in the Valve House

Thursday, February 8, 1923, was a typical winter's day — cold, blustery, and overcast. Workers at the extensive Consumers' Gas Station B on the south side of Eastern Avenue, just east of the Don River, punched the time clock and got ready for another workday.

Looking east along Eastern Avenue from Dibble Street, 2012. The three former Consumers' Gas Station B buildings adjacent to the street and visible in the old sketch still stand, though now with different tenants.

225

The morning passed as usual, with crews carrying out their normal scheduled assignments. Following a break for lunch, three of the workers entered the station's Valve House and descended to a belowground pit where they began the job of adding a new connection to an existing pipe. Nothing was unusual about the job. In fact, this type of work was done frequently as the growing city demanded additional gas, which was produced from the burning of coal in the huge ovens known as "retorts" located at the Station B plant. What was different this time would lead to a disaster — the worst in the company's long history.

As the three employees worked on installing the connection, small quantities of invisible coal gas began seeping into the below-grade pit. Within minutes the three unsuspecting workers, overcome by the fumes, slumped to the pit floor. Another member of the crew who was working on equipment on the main level wandered over to the pit and looked down to see how the work was progressing. Seeing the victims lying on the floor, he descended a ladder into the pit to offer assistance. As he did, he called for help, and others quickly arrived on the scene.

The Consumers' Gas name is visible over the entrance to Station B's 1907 office building.

STATION "B"—MANUFACTURING PLANT. EASTERN AND BOOTH AVENUES

This sketch of Consumers' Gas Station B on Eastern Avenue was prepared in 1923, the same year an industrial accident took ten lives at the plant. The tragedy occurred in the Valve House, seen in front of the huge gas holder (gasometer) to the right of the sketch.

Knowing that timing was critical, they, too, entered the pit, but one by one each would-be rescuer was overcome by the gas. Within minutes the three workers, plus all seven rescuers lay dead or dying on the pit floor. Other workers rushed to the scene to offer assistance. And as additional help from local fire halls and police stations arrived on the scene, efforts continued to breathe life into the victims. Unfortunately, it was too late. Ten Station B workers would never see another Toronto spring.

February 12, 2012

Evolution of T.O.'s Transit

One of the many things that help turn an otherwise ordinary city into a great city is the presence of a safe, reliable, affordable, and comfortable public transportation system. Toronto's commitment to excellence in public transit (though hindered in recent years as a result of political interference by people who have no expertise in "running a railway") began nearly a century ago.

Prior to the establishment of the new Toronto Transportation Commission in the fall of 1921 (the word *transportation* was replaced by *transit* coincident with the opening of the Yonge subway on March 30, 1954), public transportation had been provided for decades by private companies. First came the Wild West–style stagecoaches, then horse-drawn cars running on steel rails, and then, beginning in 1892, newfangled electric-powered street railway vehicles had citizens convinced their city was just about as modern as any city could be.

In order for these privately owned businesses to remain successful in the eyes of their directors and shareholders, profitability was "job one." Companies soon realized that the best way to achieve these obligatory financial goals was to move as many fare-paying riders as possible while forgetting, or at least downplaying, those things necessary for a safe, reliable, affordable, and comfortable service. Score one for the businessmen, zero for the public.

City of Toronto Archives.

(Above) Looking east along Danforth Avenue from just east of Pape, 1913. When opened in late 1915, the streetcars operating on the city's Toronto Civic Railway route (construction began in March 1911) served the communities along "The Danforth" between Broadview and Luttrell avenues. (Below) A similar view today.

From The Toronto Civic Railways by J. William Hood.

Passengers board one of the municipally owned Toronto Civic Railway (TCR) streetcars at the Danforth and Broadview intersection on September 28, 1920. A little less than one year later this city operated route (plus five other TCR routes) became part of the newly established Toronto Transportation Commission.

As Torontonians became more and more irritated with the way they were being treated by the street railway "barons," the public and their elected officials agreed that the optimum in public transit could only be achieved by making it the responsibility of the municipality. Attaining this goal was approved by the electorate by an overwhelming majority of 10:1 during the municipal election held January 1, 1920. The province subsequently approved the creation of the municipality's new TTC, decreeing that it would come into being on September 1, 1921.

Now, while it's true that public ownership of the city's extensive street railway system took effect on that first Thursday in September, the city had already gained some experience providing streetcar service a decade earlier, back when work began on the Toronto Civic Railway's Gerrard route that ran from Greenwood Avenue to Main Street. This city-operated service (which began on December 18, 1918) was the first to be established in response to the privately-owned Toronto Railway Company's adamant refusal to provide any public transportation on streets outside the city boundaries as they existed when the company was given its monopoly in 1891. That meant that many communities that had come into existence during the intervening years were without any form of public transportation, although they, too, were paying property taxes. The city stepped in and over the next few years the city began providing transportation to ever-increasing numbers of passengers in communities in and around Coxwell Avenue, St. Clair Avenue West, Danforth Avenue, Bloor Street West, and Lansdowne Avenue. Two of the photos accompanying this column depict the TCR's fourth project. In 1921 all six routes were absorbed into the new TTC network.

February 26, 2012

A Moving Experience

It's hard for me to believe that it was forty years ago that my wife Yarmila and I made our way to the "old" Sun Life building at 200 University Avenue where she worked. The nice security fellow then took us up to the roof, where we were able to watch as the historic Campbell House made its way west along Adelaide Street from its original location at the top of Frederick Street, then north on University Avenue to its new site at the northwest corner of Queen Street.

Sir William Campbell served as the chief justice of Upper Canada from 1825 to 1829 and was the man who built this residence in 1822. For many years the building was used as a factory for the manufacture of horseshoe nails. Photo circa 1922.

It was a special experience for the two of us (as well as for thousands of other Torontonians), especially since just a few years earlier it was pretty certain that the 150-year-old building would simply be demolished to permit the land on which it had sat since 1822 to be re-developed. (The St. James Campus of George Brown College now occupies the site).

On March 31, 1972, Campbell House was on the way from its original site on Adelaide Street East (then called Duke Street) to its new location at the northwest corner of University Avenue and Queen Street.

In an effort to preserve the old house, its owner, Coutts-Hallmark International (the latest in a long list of owners) agreed to turn the building over to the Advocate Society, a group of trial lawyers, on the condition that the structure be moved. Initial plans called for the house to be relocated to a piece of property on Simcoe Street just south of Dundas. However, subsequent discussions with the Canada Life Assurance Co. resulted in the company offering a more prominent location just to the south of its landmark head office building. The remarkable move of the two-hundred-ton structure took place on March 31 and April 1, 1972.

March 25, 2012

The Campbell House Museum today.

Getting Schooled in History

The year was 1910, and the city of Toronto was booming. In fact, with the annexation of the town of West Toronto Junction the previous year, the population had swelled to almost 350,000 (a figure many believed was actually closer to 400,000). And while the city was growing in size, in the number of citizens, and in prosperity, a mile or so north on Yonge Street the suburban town of North Toronto, located in and around the intersection of Yonge and Eglinton, was also experiencing growing pains.

Many of the citizens of the town were of the opinion that sooner or later the escalating cost of supplying water and disposing of sewage, as well as maintaining the local main roads and side streets throughout the mostly rural community, would force officials to ask the big city to the south for assistance.

Another emerging problem was the increasing concern over the schooling of the town's younger citizens, especially those looking for some post–primary school enlightenment.

To respond to this need, in the fall of 1910 town officials hired George H. Reed, a highly talented teacher who had served for twenty years as principal of the high school in Markham. Before long, Reed was busy teaching five students in a small room on the second floor of the local town hall located at the northwest corner of Yonge Street and Montgomery Avenue. The new North Toronto "high school" was up and running.

It was in a small room on the second floor of the Town of North Toronto's municipal building at Yonge Street and Montgomery Avenue that North Toronto Collegiate's very first classes were held in the fall of 1910.

North Toronto Collegiate students didn't move from the old Town Hall on Yonge Street into this, their new building on nearby Roehampton Avenue, until early in 1913.

To accommodate the increasing number of the community's young people seeking a high-school diploma, officials decided to build a proper building. So they purchased three acres of farmland north and east of the often dusty, more often muddy Yonge and Eglinton intersection. The new building was ready for students in December of 1912, by which time the anticipated annexation of the town by the City of Toronto was underway. It was about this time that the present name of the school, North Toronto Collegiate Institute, was adopted.

Numerous changes to the original building were made over the following years, but it eventually became obvious that the old structure had outlived its usefulness. After months of discussions, ground was broken in November of 2007 for the construction of a modern new school that, through an innovative financial agreement with Tridel, would result in the iconic educational facility being incorporated into a major condominium development. The "new" old North Toronto opened in September 2010.

April 1, 2012

Courtesy of Tridel.

Aerial view of the new North Toronto Collegiate Institute.

A Hot Time in Muddy York

Today when we welcome visitors to our city from south of the border, we do so with open arms. Oh, how times have changed, for it was only two hundred years ago that the only arms we extended to our neighbours were those that took the form of loaded muskets.

Captain Neal McNeale of the 8th King's Regiment was killed early in the morning of April 27, 1813, by American troops as they streamed ashore south of today's Liberty Grand (former Ontario Government Building) at the west end of Exhibition Place. This painting is by artist B.T.A. Griffiths and is from Toronto's Museum Services collection.

What has become known in the history books as the War of 1812 was a somewhat pointless conflict between the United States and Great Britain that officially began on June 18, 1812. The reasons for going to war were, in the eyes of the Americans at least, totally valid. There are numerous online sites that explain both sides of the equation. Suffice it to say that rather than iron things out peacefully, U.S. president James Madison decided to teach Great Britain a lesson and declare war, prompting an invasion of Britain's possessions in North America. This action pleased the iconic American statesman Thomas Jefferson who, on hearing the news, announced that victory over Great Britain would follow almost immediately after American troops marched into Canada. (What a weenie!) As history would confirm, it was a huge miscalculation on his part.

The war would last a grand total of 934 days, and while the treaty that ended all hostilities between the two nations was signed in the European city of Ghent on December 24, 1814, news travelled slowly. Unfortunately, that fact resulted in the deaths of several hundred troops during the totally unnecessary Battle of New Orleans, which took place a couple of weeks after the war was formally over.

American general Zebulon Pike (who in 1806 "discovered" what became known as Pike's Peak in the Rocky Mountains) was killed when the garrison's munitions magazine exploded during the April 27, 1813, attack on York (Toronto).

Since the outbreak of hostilities in the summer of 1812, things had been going extremely well for the "good guys" serving under Sir Isaac Brock, the British general who would pay with his life at the Battle of Queenston Heights in October of 1812.

However, with the arrival of spring 1813 the Americans decided it was time to flex their muscles. Plans to attack the British naval stronghold at Kingston were thwarted by weather conditions and it was decided instead to focus on the smaller, less heavily defended York, the provincial capital, with a population of six hundred or so peace-loving citizens. There's also the possibility that the mammoth British warship *Sir Isaac Brock*, still under construction there, could be captured and added to the enemy fleet. (That was not to be, as the British got to it first when things looked at their bleakest and burned it in the stocks.) Up until that time, York's citizens had been immune to the chaos and concerns brought on by the war, but on April 27, 1813, that would all change.

Streaming ashore from a fleet of U.S. navy vessels anchored off the west end of today's Exhibition Place, some 1,700 American troops were met by seven hundred valiant defenders, including a number of Mississauga, Ojibwa, and Chippewa warriors. It took some time, but the invaders eventually overran both the fort and then the town. For the next five days the American flag flew over York, after which time the invaders departed, leaving behind several burned buildings (including the young province's buildings of parliament located at the foot of Parliament Street), an empty library, and several hundred shaken citizens. Adverse winds prevented the American ships from actually leaving the town's harbour for another six days.

It was estimated that more than 180 troops from both sides were killed in the Battle of York.

Early in 2012, the bicentennial year of the War of 1812, the Ontario Heritage Trust opened the Parliament Interpretive Centre at 265 Front Street (steps west of the appropriately named Parliament Street). Located on the site of the province's first purpose-built houses of parliament, visitors to the centre can learn more about the War of 1812 and the violent attack on our community.

April 29, 2012